Praise for *Getting Over Yourself*

One of the bright young pastor stars on the horizon is my dear friend Dean Inserra. You will see why when you read this book. Wise but witty, firm but fair, convictional but cordial, he takes us on a journey through an issue that needs to be addressed for the sake of truth and the kingdom. Buckle up and enjoy the ride.

JAMES MERRITT
Senior Pastor, Cross Pointe Church, Duluth, GA

The new prosperity churches largely shun the language that we can all be wealthy if we just have more faith. The emphasis is more about experiencing God's power and presence in our lives and overcoming the lies of the enemy. The worship is upbeat and lively. This is what makes the movement, on the one hand, compelling to audiences and, on the other hand, more difficult to engage with biblical and constructive critique. This book is a surgeon's scalpel, not a cudgel. It will help the church and church leaders discern the features of a growing movement but, even more importantly, see where our own hearts may be drifting. There is wisdom here to show us how *not* to build on a foundation of sand. I've been sharpened in my commitment to build well, be faithful, and employ biblical metrics of success in gospel ministry.

MATT MASON
Pastor, The Church at Brook Hills, Birmingham, AL

A good doctor can deliver a difficult diagnosis with compassion, and Dean Inserra proves to be a faithful general practitioner for the soul. Confronting the motives and misplaced ambitions of a self-centered Christianity, this book asks, "Do I exist for God or does God exist for me?" In a culture where hostility to Christianity will only increase, there can be no more pressing need than to recover authentic discipleship. Inserra reminds us of what it means to be clay for the Potter, creature of the Creator, and servant of the Master. You may not like message of this book, but you need the message of this book.

KATIE McCOY
Assistant Professor of Theology
Theological Seminary

ist

D1473834

Pastoral brashness are not words that are supposed to go together. But Pastor Dean Inserra has carved a unique voice for lovingly critiquing the untouchable subjects of American evangelicalism without falling prey to bitter fundamentalism or therapeutized liberalism. In *Getting Over Yourself*, Dean dismantles the Instagrammification of me-focused, platform-obsessed Christianity and calls us to a deeper walk with Christ than what the Church of All the Feels can offer.

ANDREW T. WALKER
Associate Professor of Ethics, The Southern Baptist Theological Seminary

In God's providence, some books arrive at just the right time and say exactly what needs to be said. I honestly believe that is the case with *Getting Over Yourself*. Dean Inserra offers a blistering-but-biblical, withering-but-winsome critique of the new prosperity gospel. This "me-centered" vision of the Christian life is everywhere, confusing believers and stunting their spiritual maturity. In its worst forms, it presents a rival gospel to the biblical good news about the redeeming work of Jesus Christ. It tempts us all, which is why all of us need to read Dean's book. Highly recommended.

NATHAN A. FINN
Provost / Dean of the University Faculty, North Greenville University

The contents of this book lay out a way forward for anyone who wants to enjoy the freedom of following Jesus in true discipleship. For too long, many churches have settled for a shallow version of discipleship that sounds more like pop psychology than a radical call to follow Jesus. Dean offers a pathway for any disciple who wants to truly love Jesus with all of their heart, soul, mind, and strength.

JT ENGLISH
Lead Pastor, Storyline Fellowship; cohost of *Knowing Faith* podcast

Getting Over Yourself is a bold, gospel-driven, prophetic word for the American church. In reminding us of our sin and depravity, Dean reminds us of the true beauty of the gospel. The best news in the world isn't that Jesus came to Earth, lived, died, and rose again to help me live a better life. No—the best news in the all the world is that Jesus came to Earth, lived, died, and rose again to rescue me from my sinful, self-obsessed lostness to set me free to live a new life for His glory. By pointing us to the fullness of the gospel, Dean exposes the second-rate "good news" of gospel-lite, prosperity Christianity.

MARK VANCE

Lead Pastor, Cornerstone Church, Ames, IA

We live in an age where everyone is a brand and every experience is a potential marketing opportunity. Even and perhaps especially in the church. Too often Christians are tempted toward a fake gospel of soft prosperity, comfort, and self-affirmation. Dean Inserra understands that Jesus came to rescue us from the bondage of self, which is why this book is vital to put into the hands of every believer. This book carefully and surgically works through the layers of false gospels we so easily imbibe and leads us back toward a cross-centered, Christ-focused Christianity.

DANIEL DARLING

Senior VP of Communications, NRB; bestselling author of several books, including *The Characters of Christmas, A Way with Words,* and *The Dignity Revolution*

With laser-like intensity and clarity, Dean masterfully dissects the current state of much of the American church, revealing the facade of the self-centered life masquerading under the banner of Christianity and offers us Jesus, the real Jesus, in response. In the final chapter he asks, "It's clear that God is fully satisfied with Jesus. Am I?" This is the heart of the book. And it's why I think you should read it.

MICAH FRIES

Author of *Leveling the Church*; Director of Engagement, GlocalNet

Dean Inserra diagnoses a harmful but subtle trend in American Christianity where many pastors and churches have substituted a self-help hype machine baptized in Christian language for Jesus-centered discipleship. In so doing, Jesus becomes the means to your better life, not the end for whom you were created! Dean displays great bedside manner by not casting judgment, but rather showing loving concern that Christians do what we have always done since the cross and the empty tomb—get over ourselves and focus on Jesus.

JON AKIN

Director of Young Leader Engagement, North American Mission Board

Dean Inserra is one of the most down-to-earth pastors you will ever meet. He's fun, precocious, and has an incisive wit. But Dean is also a deep thinker who speaks truth in his own unique voice. *Getting Over Yourself* is the most Dean Inserra title in the world, and it so perfectly captures what the gospel is calling Christians to do—to put others before ourselves and to put Christ above all. This book will encourage you to do that.

JIMMY SCROGGINS
Lead Pastor, Family Church

In *Getting Over Yourself*, Dean Inserra tackles the me-centeredness that animates and sets the priorities of so much of church ministry in pop-Christianity. With his engaging quips and memorable phrases, he cuts to heart of the matter. We are not supposed to be "sharing the spotlight" with God. The danger of what passes for a lot of Christian teaching is that it disciples people to crave "the gifts of God." Dean rightly calls this turn of events "tragic" because it points people away from delighting in God. This, he reminds us, subverts God's vision for our lives, which is for He, Himself, to be what satisfies us (Lam. 3:24) and for us to live lives of self-denial (Mark 8:34). In this book, he sets before us some of the most common, often presumed innocuous, phrases we hear daily in pop-Christianity and challenges us to take every thought captive and continue in what we have heard and believed about God and His gospel. The issues Dean takes on in this book are not new, but in this day of such cultural and social confusion and unrest, the temptations for a me-centered Christian life are most intense. That means the arrival of this book is "just in time."

KEITH WHITFIELD
Vice President and Provost, Southeastern Baptist Theological Seminary

GETTING OVER YOURSELF

**Trading Believe-in-Yourself Religion
for Christ-Centered Christianity**

DEAN INSERRA

MOODY PUBLISHERS

CHICAGO

Unless otherwise noted, all Scripture quotations are taken from the Christian Standard Bible®, Copyright © 2017 by Holman Bible Publishers. Used by permission. Christian Standard Bible® and CSB® are federally registered trademarks of Holman Bible Publishers.

Scripture quotations marked (ESV) are from the ESV® Bible (The Holy Bible, English Standard Version®), copyright © 2001 by Crossway, a publishing ministry of Good News Publishers. Used by permission. All rights reserved.

All emphasis in Scripture has been added.

Names and details of some stories have been changed to protect the privacy of individuals.

Edited by Mackenzie Conway
Interior Design: Ragont Design
Cover design: Erik M. Peterson
Cover illustration of man copyright © 2017 by jesadaphorn / iStock (845579920). All rights reserved.

All websites and phone numbers listed herein are accurate at the time of publication but may change in the future or cease to exist. The listing of website references and resources does not imply publisher endorsement of the site's entire contents. Groups and organizations are listed for informational purposes, and listing does not imply publisher endorsement of their activities.

Library of Congress Cataloging-in-Publication Data

Names: Inserra, Dean, author.
Title: Getting over yourself : trading believe-in-yourself religion for
    Christ-centered Christianity / Dean Inserra.
Description: Chicago : Moody Publishers, [2021] | Includes bibliographical
    references. | Summary: "Getting Over Yourself is a call for Christians
    to reject the hollow messages of personal prosperity and to return to
    the humble truths of the gospel. You'll learn how to identify this
    insidious, popular theology in culture and churches and examine its
    devastating effects. You'll learn how to combat it with gospel truth
    that leads to the abundant life Jesus desires for His people"-- Provided
    by publisher.
Identifiers: LCCN 2020053388 (print) | LCCN 2020053389 (ebook) | ISBN
    9780802423078 (paperback) | ISBN 9780802499479 (ebook)
Subjects: LCSH: Christian life. | Christianity--Essence, genius, nature. |
    Faith movement (Hagin)
Classification: LCC BV4501.3 .I57 2021 (print) | LCC BV4501.3 (ebook) |
    DDC 248.4--dc23
LC record available at https://lccn.loc.gov/2020053388
LC ebook record available at https://lccn.loc.gov/2020053389

Originally delivered by fleets of horse-drawn wagons, the affordable paperbacks from D. L. Moody's publishing house resourced the church and served everyday people. Now, after more than 125 years of publishing and ministry, Moody Publishers' mission remains the same—even if our delivery systems have changed a bit. For more information on other books (and resources) created from a biblical perspective, go to: www.moodypublishers.com or write to:

Moody Publishers
820 N. LaSalle Boulevard
Chicago, IL 60610

1 3 5 7 9 10 8 6 4 2

Printed in the United States of America

To my wife, Krissie, who lives the opposite
of a self-centered faith

Contents

Introduction

I love the local church. I enjoy meeting church planters, visiting their developing churches, and offering encouragement where I can. By God's grace, the church I planted in my twenties is now an established church in our area, and I know the difficult road church planters walk. We now partner with a network of churches, which helps me connect with pastors and church leaders, and whenever I am out of town on a Sunday, I try to attend a church plant, meet the pastor and his family, and invite them to a meal after service.

One weekend, around a decade ago, my wife and I were out of town for a getaway, and we learned there was a new church from our network nearby. I'd heard positive things about the young pastor and his commitment to the Scriptures. I was excited about this church plant, which was off to a fast start, and was hopeful it would make many disciples. After visiting the church and meeting the pastor, I followed along loosely via social media and started seeing a transformation in the overall focus of his preaching over time. The message started resembling that of a motivational speaker who happened to also believe in God. Faith language was regularly used, but the focus of the preaching became the personal potential of Christians to achieve whatever they put their minds to, as long as they didn't doubt God and believed He had greater things in store for their lives.

When I first visited the church, I had seen a gospel-preaching pastor, and now he seemed more like a hype man, like a keynote

speaker brought in to motivate the sales reps at a company conference. Catchy and clever leadership quips became the approach,
and he was sounding more like the latest Instagram influencer
than the preacher of the gospel I first encountered. He was
building a brand, and it was hip, trendy, and full of—in his own
words—"favor." He was out to build a big church, and his new
approach was helping achieve that. His "followers" and Sunday
morning attendees grew significantly. If pragmatism was the
driver, he was speeding down the highway of success, pastoring a trendy and self-help-focused church, where the Bible now
seemed to be a means to the ends of self-fulfillment, realization
of personal dreams, and ambition to not settle for an average life.

I was concerned for this pastor and church, but I figured it was
somewhat isolated. However, as I began to see snippets of similar
messaging in the "church world," I found out that I was in a fairly
insulated pastor bubble with like-minded peers from like-minded
seminaries preaching biblical theology that centered on Christ.
We often hear seminary presidents and seasoned Christian leaders mention their optimism over the next generation as they see
seminary graduates head out to faithfully preach the Scriptures
and point people to a discipleship centered on God's glory in
Christ. While there is surely much to celebrate, I'm afraid that
there is a serious disparity between what is happening in seminary classrooms and what is happening in the popular Christian
world, especially among young adults and college students.

The conversations at seminary coffee shops don't reflect
the "mainstream" reality of what is gaining many followers and
drawing the attention of professing Christians around the nation.
What I saw progress at the aforementioned church plant is now
the norm in what I call the "Instagramification" of Christianity.
The trendy pastors who preach a message of personal success,

betterment, and victory are sensations on social media, and their content is streamed, watched, and followed en masse. They are celebrities, eclipsing the renown of tried and true faithful Christian leaders of history and consuming the minds of millions. This message is intoxicating to a consumeristic society—it allows one to have a theistic source of faith and an emotional connection to Jesus without the demands of biblical discipleship and conduct. It is a way to live your best earthly life, while still getting to claim Christianity.

As a pastor of a multigenerational church with a large college ministry, I started asking questions of some of our student leaders about what they were seeing amongst their peers, what pastors and churches were influential, what podcasts, books, and sermons they were listening to, etc. By a landslide, the resulting names were the carriers of the self-help and fulfillment message. Thankfully, our college ministry has been able to point students to Christ and away from this message, but it is everywhere in Christian circles and can be a barrier to connecting students. When podcasts and sermons from celebrity pastors are available on demand, some students don't want to come to church to hear a local pastor preach the Bible.

One of our most memorable and impactful student leaders, Jake, first entered our church from one of these popular churches in his former city. At first, he thought we were "mean" (his word) because we talked about sin, the need for repentance, and the necessity to get over yourself in order to follow Jesus. But because he had made some new friends at our church, he decided to stick it out for a little while, supplementing his desire for more "encouraging" sermons by listening to celebrity preacher podcasts. As Jake got connected in our church, though, he began to study theology for the first time in his small group. He started understanding the

Old Testament stories as much richer than the isolated, out-of-context, moralistic messages he had been hearing before. The gospel became more than just the thing you need to believe in order to be saved and was becoming the lens by which he was starting to see the Bible. He told me that, in his previous church exposure, the secondary benefits of the Christian faith seemed to be the point, but now he was seeing that God's glory revealed in Jesus Christ for the redemption of sinners—and being part of His mission through the local church—was what the faith was all about.

Jake reflected that in his previous church, "The benefits of the gospel were elevated as the main things to desire, rather than Christ Himself, but those benefits weren't things like holiness, justification, reconciliation, redemption, and knowing God, but rather things like confidence, 'dreams being restored' or 'learning to dream God-sized dreams,' 'victory over your giants,' and discovering your destiny and anointing." Any somewhat difficult biblical teaching was minimized, explained away, or excluded. The goal was to provide an uplifting experience, and rather than finding that in the gospel, the name of Jesus was invoked as a means to find it somewhere else. Before coming to our church, Jake certainly believed that Jesus died for his sins but was unknowingly starved for discipleship and didn't realize it until he began to encounter the real thing.

Jake's transformation from skeptic to passionate young leader is remarkable and stands out to me as a visible reminder of why it is so crucial that we do not compromise on the truth. He has now graduated and is heading into the rest of his adulthood with a palpable fire for sound doctrine and a burden to see other college students and young adults realize that God's Word is sufficient and the gospel is the greatest blessing one could ever receive. He inspires me.

I share the same concern for other pastors and Christians who have bought into the lie that Jesus came to secure for us the American Dream. Writing to the Christians in Corinth, the apostle Paul wrote, "I'm not writing this to shame you, but to warn you as my dear children" (1 Cor. 4:14). While I certainly don't have the same clout with my readers as Paul did with his, I share in his urgency and care. I do feel the need to give clarity where I see confusion. I do not write this book to shame anyone but out of a great concern for the current status of the church and the future of discipleship. My prayer is that bringing attention to what is happening in much of young adult evangelicalism (and beyond!) will help us see the need to make getting over ourselves a central aspect of the Christian life, as it always has been. I hope we can see more stories like Jake's as well-meaning believers move from a self-focused Christianity to one fueled by, centered on, and passionate about Christ. What better god than the only God, what better hope than our Savior, what better calling than the one to come, to die to ourselves, and to be with Him forever?

1

Loserville:

Is Christianity for the Cool, Trendy, and Successful?

Rarely, if ever, in the history of the church have so many firm periods slumped into commas and so many triumphant exclamation points curled into question marks.
—FRED CRADDOCK

"Christianity is for losers." I still remember the sting of offense brought on by these brash words from television tycoon Ted Turner. Not surprisingly, Turner took a lot of arrows for his comment and later apologized. It's not that Ted Turner wasn't qualified to call other people losers (although he did own the Atlanta Braves who regularly lost in postseason), but something about being publicly scorned didn't sit well with a lot of Christians, including me. Sure, his words were flippant, mocking the millions of us who have committed our lives to Christ, but I wondered if the outrage said more of us as Christians than it did of Ted Turner.

The Bible makes it clear that the gospel message is foolishness to unbelievers (1 Cor. 1:18), so why wouldn't Turner think the way he did about Christianity? His opinion wasn't unique; he simply didn't keep the thought to himself. His perspective was based on worldly evidence and criteria, which is no surprise. Is it really that scandalous for an unbelieving billionaire to view prudence and self-denial as foolish? But it turns out Turner's definition of "winning" in this life is far too similar to that of many Christians, and that's why some of us felt offended or rejected. So let's consider where Turner got it right and where he got it dead wrong. In some ways, Christians are losers. And we shouldn't be ashamed of that. But in other very real ways, we are the most victorious of all humanity.

Where Ted Got It Wrong

Christians have been given victory in Jesus Christ (1 Cor. 15:57). Victory, by definition, is not for losers. The entire premise of this book is that spiritual victory and earthly victory are not synonymous. Yet every Christian should take heart in the fact that there is no silver medal with Jesus. No second class, no JV team (sorry to middle-school me with my T-shirt that read "second place is the first loser"). Our victory in Christ summarizes the salvation experience of all who come to faith in Christ.

Jesus Christ died a substitutionary death in the place of all of those who, by faith, will repent and believe the good news of what Jesus has done for them as they are made aware of their inability to save themselves from God's just punishment of sin.

For the believer, the eternal consequences of sin are no more, and death ultimately has lost its sting (1 Cor. 15:55–56).

All followers of Jesus Christ have been "born again" (John 3:3–8), liberated from sin and death by the risen Christ, the ultimate and true winner.

Jesus Christ was indeed delivered up for our trespasses and

raised for our justification (Rom. 4:25). Jesus declared on the cross that the work He was sent to do on behalf of His people was finished. His resurrection and ascension prove that He was correct.

All who have been born again possess victory over sin's eternal consequences (separation from God and eternal death) and will one day in the new heavens and new earth have completely realized victory over sin's power. As we remain here on earth, we have the victory over sin's control, and we are now able to obey God by His powerful grace.

In short, because of Jesus, His people continue to win where it really matters.

Given these mind-bending blessings and rewards we receive because of Christ, Turner couldn't be more wrong. But there was another way in which he was right.

Where Ted Got It Right

Anthony Young, a former pitcher of the New York Mets, set the Major League Baseball record for the most consecutive losses as a starting pitcher. He earned his spot in baseball history on June 27, 1993, against the St. Louis Cardinals when for the twenty-fourth consecutive time he was the losing pitcher in a major league game.

Failing twenty-four times in a row is quite a losing streak. But think about the human condition before God. Romans 3:23 tells us that every single one of us has sinned and fallen short of the glory of God. Each of us fails an inconceivable number of times daily. Scripture tells us that apart from Christ we are "dead in our trespasses" (Eph. 2:1) and "without hope and without God in the world" (Eph. 2:12). Not the winsome, impressive bunch we'd like to be. But thankfully, and by the grace of God alone, our losing streak doesn't set the all-time record. God's free gift of His perfect Son can completely overrule it. While all have fallen short, the good for those on the losing streak is that "they are justified freely by his grace through the redemption that is in Christ Jesus" (Rom. 3:24). We come to God as failures in need of redemption, not as self-sufficient winners. But once in Christ, we are secure in our victory in Him. He will not drop us. He will not miss. He will not be overcome.

Why This Matters

Ted Turner was not referring to the work of Jesus when he called Christianity a religion for losers, but he was onto something especially poignant for our current cultural climate. Something has shifted in American Christian culture. The "Jesus" of some American Christians has changed. For many, He's no longer the Lamb of God who takes away the sins of the world, or the Word present at creation and who now reigns over all, or the unique Son of God, co-eternal with the Father. Instead He has become a personal life coach, sent to help us be winners rather than losers in this world.

> **Once in Christ, we are secure in our victory in Him. He will not drop us. He will not miss. He will not be overcome.**

To many professing Christians, Jesus has become a success guru who dispenses positive thoughts to help them get the next big promotion. The victories this Jesus gives do not involve overcoming sin, but rather come through the lens of the American Dream: success, empowerment, motivation, and personal fulfillment. These ambitions have become a central focus for many North American Christians. That's why we want to jump to our own defense when we're called losers and point to lives that look just as successful and shiny as the world. We want to be able to have Jesus *and* the career, the finances, the body, and the influence of those who are "winning" in this life.

How Did We Get Here?

I'm afraid a look into popular Christianity in America reveals teachings of a religion far from what the early church would have recognized. This Christianity worships a god who wants us to achieve worldly happiness, make our dreams prosper, and reach our fullest potential, proving people like Ted Turner wrong in the name of Jesus. We have largely set aside dated "prosperity gospel" preachers in fancy suits and gaudy television studio sets, yelling into a camera with a phone number to call at the bottom of the screen to receive a special blessing or prayer cloth. This kind of instant health-and-wealth teaching is now a fringe movement, more broadly mocked than followed. But in its place is a new prosperity gospel carried into the mainstream by trendy, attractive, compelling speakers.

This new teaching (which I'll call "pop-Christianity" or "new prosperity theology") is not centered on overnight rags-to-riches stories or immediate physical healing, but rather on the idea that God is "in my corner" waiting to give me my "breakthrough." The new prosperity gospel comes with the message of "God-sized dreams" and a "vision" that God has for your life, which includes finding your "destiny" and "reaching your true potential." No longer is our depravity the actual tragedy. Now, the cardinal sin is failing to achieve "God's best" for oneself. Instead of standing on the character of God, the focus is now to lay claim to "greater things," because if God really loves us and if He's as powerful as He claims to be, then "the best is yet to come." It's not difficult to see why it is so appealing!

There's truth to some of these platitudes, which is why we have to be careful. And that's what makes them so dangerous. If we're not careful, we can turn legitimate confidence in our victory in Christ into the idea that God wants us to walk in earthly victory as we define it for ourselves. It's certainly true that God cares greatly about our well-being and wants to give us abundant life (John 10:10). But so often the way we perceive blessing and victory is not the same as the Bible's definitions of blessing and victory. And the American church has largely fallen prey to the idea that God being "for our good" means God is for our worldly good.

From the first pages of Scripture, we see God's people fail to live in light of God's sovereignty and provision. In the book of Exodus, the recently rescued Israelites crave the comforts of captivity in Egypt over the hardships of freedom in the desert. New Testament churches had bouts with false teachers, and churches throughout the modern era have fallen into various traps as well. This one is our generation's trap—a fully-fledged "me-focused" faith of which I'm afraid we haven't even yet seen the long-term effects. And we shouldn't be complacent. Throughout Scripture, God never applauds or excuses His people's idolatry. He corrects it. Consistently. Painfully.

> **It's certainly true that God cares greatly about our well-being and wants to give us abundant life (John 10:10). But so often the way we perceive blessing and victory is not the same as the Bible's definitions of blessing and victory.**

Pastor Ray Ortlund is quoted as saying, "Christianity shows us something profound. Moment by moment, we are either centered on God or we are centered on ourselves. There is no alternative."[1]

To follow Jesus is to deny oneself (Matt. 16:24) rather than seek one's personal elevation. The easiest litmus test I can think of for evaluating the competing messages heard in churches nationwide is this: Is the message promoting or rejecting a "for you" theology? While I certainly hope and believe that all orthodox theology is *for* us, in terms of receiving the truth of Scripture and its significance for our lives, the "for you" message is an unofficial theology that functions as if God's reason for existence is . . . *you.*

Is God's primary business making sure you are able to fulfill your greatest longings? Is God's main goal helping you reach your "potential" via notoriety, worldly comfort, personal happiness, or achievements? Do we measure God's faithfulness by how often He behaves like a personal genie? Do I exist for God or does God exist for me?

Apart from being unbiblical, a theology centered on one's own individual desires and comfort is unrealistic for most of the world. Even in a first-world context, not everyone can pursue the career or lifestyle of their choice and see nothing but success. These faulty applications of Scripture's victory stories allow professing Christians to feel justified in valuing the things they lusted over prior to conversion and in viewing Jesus as the perfect cheerleader along the way. But this is the new era of the Western church, and it is in the mainstream of popular Christianity. I'm afraid many haven't yet realized the significance of this shift.

> **It is impossible to deny oneself until you get over yourself.**

The reality is: Most Christians in America simply aren't okay with being "the least of these." We don't want to be losers, when in reality we should be the least afraid of failure. If we are truly in Christ, we are certainly now winners in the eyes of God but are guaranteed to be losers in the eyes of the world (John 15:18–19). This is part of the cost of being the people of God. We cannot worship both God and the things of this world.

It is impossible to deny oneself until you get over yourself. There is something so much better that God has for His people, and winning in this world is not what He has in mind.

2

The Shenanigans:

What Goes On Inside a New Prosperity Church

"This is the church, and this is the steeple.
Open the doors, and see all the people."

You won't find "New Prosperity Church of [Your Hometown]" on any church marquee. To understand how a new prosperity gospel infiltrated American Christianity, one must look inside the churches and evaluate the message and the messengers of this new ideology. I want to make very clear at the start that this book addresses some nuanced material and therefore will require some patience and grace on your part. First, I think there are false teachers in the church at large, promoting a message to which I am fervently opposed and about which I am genuinely concerned. Second, I think these popular pastors can influence otherwise well-meaning pastors and leaders of other churches. Third, I think many Christians have been misled and don't have the tools to properly discern whether the message they're hearing is in line with biblical theology. Last, all of us have sinful human tendencies we must war against on a daily basis—tendencies to view ourselves as the center of every situation. Given all of those factors, this book is both a vehement rejection of a false gospel and a heartfelt exhortation for each of us to look for seeds of new prosperity fruit growing in our own hearts. The problem simply isn't "out there." It's inside us, too.

Many popular American churches offer an incredible experience. In fact, many churches are open about the fact that this is their goal, to the extent that they even call their worship gatherings by that name, "experiences." I am not trying to raise alarm about the various naming conventions for church programming, but it is essential to understand the new emphasis on creating compelling experiences. To many, creating an experience is the point of the gathering. I know pastors who did not want to return to having church gatherings once restrictions were lifted during COVID-19, simply because they knew they couldn't provide the same experience because of social distancing guidelines and a smaller attendance. Why is this more important than the church simply coming together after months of being prevented from doing so? Open the doors, and you will see that the greater the personal felt experience, the more bought-in the spectators.

Imagine attending a national convention or annual meeting for a multilevel marketing (MLM) wellness company that sells some sort of health supplement for weight loss or "clean living." Simply follow someone on social media involved in those types of companies and you will see every motivational self-help quote imaginable. I have nothing against MLMs, but if just that one person you follow is really intense, it is not surprising to think of what happens when hundreds or thousands of the top sellers come together from across the country for a conference. It is certainly an experience. Combine a pep rally in an arena with a celebrity self-help guru speaker, and you get the picture. The ambitious entre-preneurial wellness champions leave the convention fired up and ready to take on the world, and your social media feed will feel the results. You'll be flooded with messaging about making changes in your life and being a better you. They had a "life-changing" week-end, and now they are going to help you experience the same—if you just join their team, buy their product, and take the road to the personal happiness that you are told you deserve.

Take away the meal supplement shakes and tack on some Bible verses to these kinds of gatherings, and you have a glimpse of new prosperity gospel churches. Rather than having that mo-tivational Monday and achieving your set goals as you "get after it," Jesus is the one to help you live your best life. The unofficial theme of these church services is HYPE, as keeping people ex-cited and optimistic will allow them to enjoy the Sunday expe-rience and keep coming back for more. The pastor is never offen-sive and always inspiring. These pastors are often elite com-municators with fashion sense that would make an Instagram influencer look like a picture in an Olan Mills church directory.

> **Take away the meal supplement shakes and tack on some Bible verses to these kinds of gatherings, and you have a glimpse of new prosperity gospel churches.**

Martyn Lloyd-Jones, speak-ing in the mid-twentieth century, once voiced that the main trou-ble in the church was the "appalling superficiality." Sadly, I don't think we've outgrown his concerns. If anything, it's gotten much worse. In the new prosperity gospel churches, there isn't just a message, but also a style. Appearance matters a great deal, and the faces of these churches must meet certain standards of attractiveness and fashion in order to be on the "platform." Theologian Carl Trueman described this sort of influential movement as having "savvy harnessing of fashionable idioms and marketing strategies, exceptionally clever use of social media . . . all fronted by attractive personalities and brilliant communicators."[1]

The messaging plays to the emotions and the deep individualism of our culture, emphasizing each hearer's "journey" and "story." The new prosperity gospel message is consistently all about you:

> Dream God-sized dreams—God has a vision for your life.
> Discover your destiny.
> God wants to turn your setback into a comeback.
> God has something greater for you.
> You have untapped potential that God wants to unleash.
> The best is yet to come.

These sound like the halftime pep talks from a high school football coach looking for anything to motivate his tired players to come back and win. Instead, they are the captions and sound bites upon which entire sermon series are built. To be fair, some of this on the preacher side and much of it on the congregant side can be attributed to biblical illiteracy and not vicious intentions. These things all sound good because we can think of a time God used someone, somewhere in a similar fashion. Unfortunately, these aren't actual promises in the Scriptures but mere examples of unique and isolated events involving characters from the Bible distorted to move the focus from God the conqueror, God the provider, God the creator to us as the champions of every story. Not only are the vague promises of the new prosperity gospel insufficient to equip us for godly living, they are also inapplicable to most humans around the world, not the least of which are our Christian brothers and sisters suffering actual persecution globally.

Instead of the health-and-wealth message of late-night Christian television, the new prosperity gospel centers on self-actualization and self-worth, wrapped in a Sunday morning pep rally where the gospel of self-fulfillment is preached with passion. Trevin Wax describes this self-centered gospel as one where the message is "to discover and express your unique sense of self, no matter what others may say or do to challenge your freedom of personality. The narrative arc of your life is finding your personal route to happiness by following your heart, expressing your true self, and then fighting whoever would oppose you—your society, your family, your past, or your church." He goes on to claim that "this is one of the dominant narratives of our time. It shows up in movies and music, and increasingly, on the platforms of popular preachers and teachers—both male and female."[2] That quote struck me. Movies and music? Yes, that makes perfect sense for the world, but notice who was also included in Wax's description, "preachers."

In their sermons, these preachers often include (but misuse) Bible verses and Christian concepts, tweaking the application just enough to make it easy to nod in agreement rather than ask how the message is compatible with the life of following Jesus that is presented in the Bible. In new prosperity churches, Christian terminology is often repackaged in a way that redirects congregants toward their own stories and away from self-denial, picking up a cross, and living to magnify Jesus above all.

Wax gives examples of this repackaging:

> Sin is failing to reach your potential.
> Shame is a subjective feeling you bring upon yourself and must set aside, not a state that results from objective sin against a holy God.
> Guilt is what happens when you fail to accept yourself, to love yourself, or to sense your own worthiness of happiness.
> The barriers that stand in your way of pursuing your dreams must all come down, no matter where they are.[3]

This is the Disney-fication of the Bible: When you believe in Jesus, He makes all your dreams come true. Yes, Jesus saves you from your sins, but He's also like the genie from *Aladdin*.

To be fair, just because a preacher proclaims the gospel of self-fulfillment doesn't mean he never preaches the truth. There is great skill in speaking just enough truth that one can miss the important omissions or alterations. In Jude's short New Testament letter, he warned us these matters can creep in "unnoticed" (Jude 4 ESV). Theologian Conrad Mbewe said that these preachers "often use scriptural words but fill them with wrong meanings and interpretations. Only well-taught minds will be able to pick that up and reject the error."[4]

Of course, it is true that God doesn't want His people to remain in our guilt and shame, and He tells us we are now new creations in Christ (2 Cor. 5:17). That new life He has given us, however, was never designed for Christians to flourish by the standards of this world, where self-fulfillment is the chief value, but rather to make spiritually dead people alive, forgive us of our sins, and begin the long process of making us more like Jesus as we join God on His mission of taking the gospel to the world. It is not my plans that need to be actualized but God's Word in my life.

By His grace and sovereign will, God is working all things together for our good—not for our personal dreams, but for His dream for His people: to make us more like Jesus (Rom. 8:28–29). When you open the door and see all the people of God's church, the actual journey He has for His children is one to conform us to the likeness of Christ. This is God's ambition. It translates to every tongue, tribe, and nation and should be the actual "God-sized dream" we want for our lives.

> By His grace and sovereign will, God is working all things together for our good, not for our personal dreams, but for His dream for His people: to make us more like Jesus.

3

What's the Hype?
The Draw of Worldly Christianity

The New Testament Church was identified
with persecutions, prisons, and poverty;
today many of us are identified with
prosperity, popularity, and personalities.
—LEONARD RAVENHILL

"I don't get the hype," my friend said about the new restaurant
opening in our city.

"Seriously?" I asked. I'd been unofficially counting down the
days until opening, waiting for the renowned barbeque joint to
open its Tallahassee outpost. We were getting hometown access
to the Tom Brady of ribs and my buddy didn't "get the hype." As
former UCLA basketball coach John Wooden would say, "Goodness gracious sakes alive."

On the drive back from our inaugural lunch, I asked my friend
what he thought about the food itself and he casually said, "It was
fine. I just don't really get the appeal."

In this instance, my friend was beginning with a severe

skepticism that even delicious barbeque couldn't overcome. On the other hand, I was beginning with high expectations, which were bound to either lead to extreme disappointment or a biased impression of what was put onto my plate. In either case, we were both in for a confrontation between expectation and reality. But the sort of excited optimism I had comes close to what we're seeing amongst antsy, searching people and a prosperity gospel that promises a God whose chief goal is to facilitate your personal happiness. It's not hard to find the appeal.

We all feel pressure to pursue peace with God, whether that means reasoning away His existence or seeking to appease whatever version of Him we think exists. That's part of the issue with the new prosperity gospel. Whereas the Bible teaches that peace with God comes via death (to Christ and also to self), this newer message implies that peace with God is settled, and we can now return to the preeminent goal of self-fulfillment. The ultimate appeal is that you can pursue the earthly carrots dangling in front of you in the name of Christianity.

As author Jen Pollock Michel rightly noted, our society believes that "happiness is our only duty today, self-betrayal our only sin."[1] This version of Christianity functionally gives a hearty "amen." In a therapeutic society, the achievement of self-fulfillment with God's apparent stamp of approval is the perfect recipe for Christians to desire the things of this world while still feeling as if they are close to Jesus and He is very pleased. It appeases our need to know God isn't mad at us while giving us license to continue on making much of ourselves.

But the Scriptures give a condition to following Jesus that is the complete opposite of self-pursuit: self-denial. Jesus said, "Whoever does not bear his own cross and come after me cannot be my disciple" (Luke 14:27). My mentor puts it this way:

"Salvation is free, but following
Jesus isn't cheap." Being part of
God's kingdom means I am not
the one in charge, and sometimes the boss and I are going
to have different ideas. Imagine
following Jesus without having
to renounce yourself? This version of Jesus would always want

> **The ultimate appeal
> is that you can pursue
> the earthly carrots
> dangling in front of
> you in the name of
> Christianity.**

for me exactly what I want for myself—in the same manner I want
it for myself but with supernatural powers to make it happen.
Unfortunately, that's just not who the Bible portrays Jesus to
be. As Mark Sayers said, the "heresy hidden under the surface
is our belief that God would not ask Western people to deny
themselves."[2]

I'm not implying that new prosperity gospel churches are
flooded with raging egomaniacs. In fact, many of the people in
these churches are passionate about social justice issues, generous
with their time and resources, and truly bought-in to their local
churches. My use of the term "me-centered" refers to the focus of
the theological teaching. Think of the solar system. Humans once
believed the earth was at the center of the universe with the sun
and stars orbiting around it. We now understand that is not true in
the slightest. (At least I hope everyone reading this understands
that.) The primary error of the new prosperity theology is that it
places the individual in the center of every situation and places
God in orbit as a sort of powerful yet controllable satellite.

One popular pastor has written, "If the size of your vision for
your life isn't intimidating to you, there's a good chance it's insult-
ing to God."[3] This pastor claims God "intends to uproot you from
the tyranny of the familiar, shatter the monotonous life you've

had, and take you on an adventure."[4] I can hear the cheers of thousands at the MLM national conference, giving each other a high-five and wanting more. This same pastor wrote, "The greater life hasn't ended for you. It's only out of sight under the waters of the ordinary. And God can resurface it, supernaturally, as many times as it takes. As many times as you're willing."[5] For a society living in chronic discontent, it's easy to see why this attracts people like the "Hot Now" sign at Krispy Kreme. How can you not stop in for the hot donut?

> **The primary error of the new prosperity theology is that it places the individual in the center of every situation and places God in orbit as a sort of powerful-yet-controllable satellite.**

Perhaps one of the most alarming characteristics of this movement is the genuine and seemingly powerful emotional buy-in of the people involved. "God showing up" to a gathering means people were really into the music and responded with excitement to the pastor's message about overcoming whatever obstacle is in the way of one's dream.[6] In new prosperity gatherings, conviction is usually not tied to realizing one's sin, but rather to realizing you're not being as proactive in pursuing self-care, positive thinking, or ambition as those on stage.

Congregants are made to believe they have to "listen to [them]selves, to behave authentically, in tune with what [their] intuition dictates,"[7] which is apparently God Himself calling them to something greater. Be careful what drives your emotion and in which direction! In pop-Christianity, people claim they are elevating God; they just functionally believe that is done by emoting passionately during the service to "give everything to

Him." Me-centered Christianity is very expressive, but we must take great care as to the content of the worship, because "quite possibly, the worst judgement on this side of heaven is to be under the delusion that you are worshipping God, when in reality you are only worshipping a god you created."[8]

Bob Dylan once sang about how so many of us act like God is our errand boy.[9] How many of us subconsciously view God in that way? Even Jesus Himself, God's grace and glory in bodily form, met people who just didn't want what He was offering unless He catered to their perceived needs. But it was not Jesus' duty to cater to them. In John's gospel, there is a well-known story of Jesus giving people exactly what they wanted in a meal to satisfy their hunger. John's account sets the stage by letting us know why so many people at the time were interested in Jesus and following Him: "A huge crowd was following him because they saw the signs that he was performing by healing the sick" (John 6:2). Jesus was doing amazing things:

> So when Jesus looked up and noticed a huge crowd coming toward him, he asked Philip, "Where will we buy bread so that these people can eat?" He asked this to test him, for he himself knew what he was going to do.
>
> Philip answered him, "Two hundred denarii worth of bread wouldn't be enough for each of them to have a little."
>
> One of his disciples, Andrew, Simon Peter's brother, said to him, "There's a boy here who has five barley loaves and two fish—but what are they for so many?"
>
> Jesus said, "Have the people sit down."
>
> There was plenty of grass in that place; so they sat down. The men numbered about five thousand. Then Jesus took the loaves, and after giving thanks he distributed them to those

who were seated—so also with the fish, as much as they wanted. (John 6:5–11)

Jesus gives His disciples continued evidence of His deity and power by giving more than five thousand people more food than they could even eat! Jesus saw a need, met the need, and made His greatness and power known. He could do the miraculous and unexplainable, as God in the flesh. If I saw someone feed an entire amphitheater full of people with just a few Chick-fil-A sandwiches, I would either think I was under an illusion at a magic show, or, as I took a bite and realized that the food was real, I would get up immediately and ask him to do more things for me. This would be someone worth following, even worshiping, if he was really God. The appeal would be great—he just fed thousands Chick-fil-A and didn't have the event catered.

John says that, "when the people saw the sign [Jesus] had done, they said, 'This truly is the Prophet who is to come into the world'" (John 6:14). The crowd tried to follow Jesus to ask how they, too, could perform great works (John 6:28), but Jesus saw their motives. "Truly I tell you, you are looking for me, not because you saw the signs, but because you ate the loaves and were filled. Don't work for the food that perishes but for the food that lasts for eternal life, which the Son of Man will give you, because God the Father has set his seal of approval on him" (John 6:26–27).

They wanted to follow Jesus because the earthly benefits seemed incredible. Not only that, but maybe they, too, could become great. Jesus wasn't having it. He knew that the appeal to them was not Himself but the perks. They didn't want to pick up a cross but a magic wand. Jesus then shared the good news with them by telling them what God sees as the great work: "Jesus re-plied, 'This is the work of God—that you believe in the one he has sent'" (John 6:29). Not Jesus the dream-giver, but Jesus the Savior of sinners. But this wasn't enough:

> "What sign, then, are you going to do so that we may see and believe you?" they asked. "What are you going to perform? Our ancestors ate the manna in the wilderness, just as it is written: He gave them bread from heaven to eat."
>
> Jesus said to them, "Truly I tell you, Moses didn't give you the bread from heaven, but my Father gives you the true bread from heaven. For the bread of God is the one who comes down from heaven and gives life to the world." (John 6:30–33)

"What sign are you going to perform?" Insert eye-roll emoji. Jesus had just fed more than five thousand people from a boy's lunchbox, and they wanted a sign? They still assumed that the blessing of God was more "stuff," pointing to physical food from the Hebrews in the wilderness with Moses, when Jesus wanted them to see their spiritual needs, the true hunger that needed to be addressed. Then they said, "Sir, give us this bread always," without realizing He was not referring to unlimited breadsticks at Olive Garden, but Himself. Jesus answered that He is the food they truly need, and foreshadowed His own death, stating:

> "Truly I tell you, anyone who believes has eternal life. I am the bread of life. Your ancestors ate the manna in the wilderness, and they died. This is the bread that comes down from heaven so that anyone may eat of it and not die. I am the living bread that came down from heaven. If anyone eats of this bread he will live forever. The bread that I will give for the life of the world is my flesh." (John 6:47–51)

The manna given to their ancestors was temporary. Yes, it was important, and God provided it for His people, but the people ate it for a while and still died. Here is Jesus offering them the greatest "perk" one could ever imagine—eternal life with God Himself—and that simply wasn't the answer they were looking for.

Jon Bloom aptly wrote, "Jesus was a hero to the crowd because he had fed them. But Jesus discerned something very wrong about their enthusiasm. They wanted more 'bread from heaven' (John 6:32). But wanting the blessings Jesus provides is not the same thing as believing in him."[10] This is what Jesus is getting to and trying to help them understand. In following verses, Jesus tells the crowd that they must eat His flesh and drink His blood. He is the sustenance of life. That'll shoo away a crowd any day. Bloom explains, "For Jesus, eating is *believing*; drinking is *believing*. He promises eternal life to those who believe in him."[11] What does this mean?

Jesus points us to the fact that "his death—the breaking of his body and spilling of his blood—pays in full the penalty for our sin, and that his perfect righteousness is freely given to us in exchange for our unrighteousness."[12] The crowds were disappointed. They wanted signs, power, on-demand bread from heaven; not whatever Jesus was talking about. They hit the road, filled temporarily but soon to be hungry again. Sadly, the one who could feed them in a way they never hoped or imagined was standing right in front of them, offering Himself.

I don't want to be remotely unfair and suggest that those in pop-Christian circles don't believe Jesus is the bread of life. My concern is that that isn't enough. It's not the draw of the movement. Too often, people are looking for the signs and wonders. Jared C. Wilson wrote a stern and sobering warning about these pastors who appeal to so many: "Woe to those whose ministry hallmarks amount to their fashion sense and fantastical teaching. A huge bill is coming due."[13] If the appeal is more than Jesus as Himself, my fear is we will eventually see another crowd walk away.

4

Hashtag Filter:

The Promise of the Socially Approved Life

In the world, you find peace when you embrace
your true self. In the Bible, you find peace
when you embrace Jesus the true human.
—OWEN STRACHAN

*I need to tuck my shirt in just right so when I walk down the hallway
everyone can see the tag on the back of my shorts*: This was a regular
thought in my mind as a thirteen-year-old getting dressed for
school. It was the early 1990s and wearing Duck Head shorts was
a very big deal to the throng of voice-cracking, braces-wearing
adolescents I would be seeing in the halls. I'm sure Duck Head
shorts were no different than any other shorts I could've gotten
for much cheaper (sorry, Mom and Dad), but having the right
clothes was extremely important to socially survive at my afflu-
ent suburban middle school. The proper way to demonstrate your
mastery of the style was to tuck in your shirt so the yellow Duck
Head tag on the belt loop would shine for all to see. For the first

time in my life, I was in favor of tucking in my shirt, as Mom had always wanted. Whatever it took for everyone else to see the tag.

Admittedly, I still have my preferred brands as an adult, but now with children of my own, I see how ridiculous and superficial I was as a young teen. I hope my kids don't have their thoughts preoccupied with what others think about them or make their primary goal to obtain the world's stamp of approval. I find myself most worried for them because I still struggle with seeking approval from others, though perhaps no longer by flaunting a tag on my belt loop. My seventh grade Duck Head self hasn't gone away, but he now allows other social pressures to dictate many of my choices, associations, and actions. Between "Christian Twitter," denominational associations, and the general social pressures of being a human in the 2020s, we need to be constantly aware of our tendency to lean toward thoughts like these:

> Did enough people like my social media post? Maybe I should have used a better filter.
>
> Am I viewed as impressive or successful? I hope the crowd really turns out at church on Sunday. I should probably retweet some compliments given to me. I'll include that I'm "humbled" by them, so it doesn't look like I'm bragging.
>
> God wants me to have a bigger platform than this, I just know it. Hope it doesn't look like I'm settling.
>
> Do people admire my marriage and parenting? I should post more dramatic captions about my love for my wife when I post a selfie from us on a date.
>
> Does our family look perfect in the latest photo from the beach? I should have sucked in my belly a little more and had the kids wear something trendier.

While it is easy to get stuck in what others think, I can also find myself just as consumed with how I feel personally in any given moment. My comfort, happiness, and the quality of my experiences can cause me to expect others—and even God—to cater to my desires. The only solution to these fleshly moments for me is Christian discipleship through the Holy Spirit, pointing me back to something better through God's Word: the promise of God's commitment to make me more like Jesus and have me share in His life. This is the opposite of getting that perfect tuck-in so everyone can see that I'm a big deal.

I mention this because I want to emphasize that all of us are afflicted with the tendency to forget Christ. However, biblical community should not be a place that fosters those tendencies. I fear that unlike biblical counsel, which points us away from ourselves and to the sufficiency of Christ, new prosperity churches are encouraging followers to wade deeper and more doggedly into their own personal concerns.

In Philippians 3, Paul asserts that Christians show immaturity by being consumed with the matters of the world. He instead characterizes maturity by focusing pursuit on things above: "I pursue as my goal the prize promised by God's heavenly call in Christ Jesus. Therefore, let all of us who are mature think this way" (Phil. 3:14–15). Mature Christians are focused on a different prize. We care about what people think of us only in terms of how it represents Jesus (Matt. 5:16–17). Paul continues:

> And if you think differently about anything, God will reveal this also to you. In any case, we should live up to whatever truth we have attained. Join in imitating me, brothers and sisters, and pay careful attention to those who live according to the example you have in us. For I have often told you, and

now say again with tears, that many live as enemies of the cross of Christ. Their end is destruction; their god is their stomach; their glory is in their shame; and they are focused on earthly things. Our citizenship is in heaven, and we eagerly wait for a Savior from there, the Lord Jesus Christ. He will transform the body of our humble condition into the likeness of his glorious body, by the power that enables him to subject everything to himself. (Phil. 3:15–21)

> I fear that unlike biblical counsel, which points us away from ourselves and to the sufficiency of Christ, new prosperity churches are encouraging followers to wade deeper and more doggedly into their own personal concerns.

Either we are going to be focused on heavenly things, or we are going to be focused on this world and ourselves. Focusing on Christ and His mission should make us feel like a fish out of water in this life as we pursue different dreams, different goals, different desires, and a different God than those of this world. This is the process of becoming more like Jesus.

"If you have been raised with Christ, seek the things above, where Christ is, seated at the right hand of God. Set your minds on things above, not on earthly things. For you died, and your life is hidden with Christ in God" (Col. 3:1–3). One cannot be an effective disciple of Jesus Christ and be self-consumed or fixated on earthly things.

One of my biggest concerns with the new prosperity gospel is that it suggests we should want the same things after our

Christian conversion that we desired before we knew Christ. These are usually not the visible "big sins" but the more subtle sins of self-satisfaction, self-focus, self-absorption, etc. How do these sins pass as "Christian" virtues? The new prosperity gospel preaches them as such. The result is a belief that, in order to be truly happy, we need more than what God has already given us. In other words, the unspoken implication is that Jesus isn't enough—He's a means to an end.

I've found that the new prosperity gospel emphasizes "not settling for less than God's best," but that "best" is rarely being conformed into the likeness of Christ. "Putting God first" is believed to be important, but only because then it is assumed that God will put us first and our pursuits of self-fulfillment seem to be a Christian activity. After all, we're "giving God the glory," right?

It is important to understand that many disciples of the new prosperity gospel may genuinely want to love and follow Jesus; they just haven't realized that they are being discipled by a form of Moralistic Therapeutic Deism (MTD) rather than the faith that was "delivered to the saints once for all" (Jude 3). MTD is described as seeing God as a cosmic therapist and divine butler, ready to help out when needed.[1] To marry this to the new prosperity gospel is to see God as a genie to be sung to passionately as He leads you out of a mundane rut and into your best life. Brian Cosby, a Tennessee pastor, claims that MTD's "preacher is American entitlement" and "its sermon is a me-centered message about a distant, therapeutic god who wants [me] to be good and happy."[2] I am convinced that people have bought into this line of thinking not because they have *misunderstood* what the church has taught them but because this is the *actual message* of their churches, authors, and favorite pastors to follow on Instagram.

In *The Gospel According to Satan,* Jared C. Wilson centers on some unofficial mantras of modern day pop-Christianity. Notice how entwined the Christian-sounding phrases have become with the others in the list that people with no acknowledgment of God could also get behind:

God just wants you to be happy.
You only live once.
You need to live your truth.
Your feelings are reality.
Your life is what you make it.
You need to let go and let God.[3]

> To marry this to the new prosperity gospel is to see God as a genie to be sung to passionately as He leads you out of a mundane rut and into your best life.

The very popular *Jesus Calling* devotional is on the desks and in the backpacks of millions of people who have no idea how slippery the slope is. Though it makes much of Jesus, it ascribes to Him an almost fortune cookie–like voice and aims to soothe the reader with an imagined characterization of what Jesus might be like instead of pointing to the biblical evidence for God's love in Christ. For example, one of the devotionals begins: "This is a time in your life when you must learn to let go: of loved ones, of possessions, of control."[4] Another begins, "You can achieve the victorious life through living in deep dependence on Me. . . . This is not a path of continual success but of multiple failures. However, each failure is followed by a growth spurt."[5] While it isn't heretical, it is dangerously extra-biblical if the reader isn't familiar with biblical teaching.

The author claims that she "yearned for something more" than the Bible. "Increasingly, I wanted to hear what God might want to communicate to me on a given day. I decided to 'listen' with pen in hand, writing down whatever I 'heard' in my mind."[6] Why would Bible-believing people embrace a book that claims the Bible wasn't scratching an itch for the author? Because the same is true of those reading it. It's as if we're saying, "Jesus isn't enough. But He's necessary to unlock whatever *would* be enough for me." In many cases, this might not stem from a place of ambition but rather from a need to be soothed and reassured that we are on good terms with God.

Kenda Creasy Dean, in her book *Almost Christian,* claims MTD has "little to do with God or a sense of a divine mission in the world. It offers comfort, bolsters self-esteem, [and] helps solve problems."[7] Pastor and author Brian Cosby asks us to "think about those three words, Moralistic Therapeutic Deism." He rightly states that they "run counter to the gospel of Jesus Christ in every way." God is not the "divine genie dispensing wishes at command . . . but the personal Immanuel who became man to seek and save his bride. . . . Jesus has accomplished for you—through his life, death, and resurrection—everything that God has required of you; thereby, securing eternal life for all God's people, and received by faith alone."[8] If only this was enough for those who claim His name.

"American Christianity has become a 'generous host' to this low-commitment, entertainment-driven model of ministry,"[9] and the results for the future of discipleship should cause great concern. How does one stay walking with Jesus and participating in His life when things don't work out as promised or planned? The prosperity spin on the Christian faith has to be exhausting. Yet Jesus said His yoke is easy and His burden is light (Matt. 11:30).

As Michael Reeves writes, "When your culture is hedonistic, your religion therapeutic, and your goal a feeling of personal well-being, fear will be the ever-present headache."[10] A powerful or emotional experience won't do the trick when one suddenly realizes that God's "vision for my life" might not be fame, comfort, and self-actualization.

Pastor Rusty McKie reminds us that it is not "the occasional, breathtaking moments of connecting with Jesus that lead to sustained kingdom joy—although we thank God for them. It's decades of obedience through ordinary spiritual disciplines that lead us into the extraordinary life Jesus promised."[11] We know unbelieving celebrities have bemoaned the surprising disappointment of achieving unthinkable worldly success and finding no true fulfillment. Now imagine feeling that deflating sadness when your anticipation was also tied to your belief in God's character and faithfulness. I worry for a generation of Christians who have tied their dreams and ambitions to a Christian experience that has nothing to do with the actual Christianity we see in the Scriptures. It will be a sobering day when God is held to promises He never actually made to His people.

The path of following Jesus is one of joys and sorrows, of mountaintop moments and heartbreaking awareness of the reality of the broken world. One cannot be made more like Christ if he or she wants to be more like this world. English Puritan John Flavel wrote about the much better life for the believer: "The intent of the Redeemer's undertaking was not to purchase for his people riches, ease, and pleasures on earth; but to

> **It will be a sobering day when God is held to promises He never actually made to His people.**

mortify their lusts, heal their natures, and spiritualize their affections; and thereby to fit them for the eternal fruition of God."[12] God's vision for our lives is Himself. How tragic that God's design (the local church) has become a factory for unbiblical teaching that points people away from that vision rather than right into it.

5

This Is So Boring:

The New Prosperity Cardinal Sin of Settling for the Mundane

Do you think God would make us so dissatisfied with this world if He did not mean to satisfy us with another and a better one?
—CHARLES SPURGEON

As a pastor who has done a lot of marital crisis counseling, I can report that Instagram regularly presents false realities about relationships. However, when it comes to smelling trouble, it rarely lies. The following scenario (between two fictionalized characters) is all too common:

Jenny is a married stay-at-home mom. Until recently, her social media posts were usually pictures of her family, pictures of vacation, and an occasional post of a new purchase or outfit for the kids. Over a few months, those posts went away, replaced by daily selfies of a tanned and slender Jenny. Her posts began to come with inspirational captions, such as

"You are worth it" and "Do more of what makes you happy." She seems to have a lot of confidence in her new appearance and wants the world to see. Slowly, but noticeably, her husband and kids are mentioned less and less, replaced by pictures from her workout or her martini from a girls' night. The evenings out seem to be a couple nights a week.

As an onlooker (and, again, someone with a lot of experience counseling troubled marriages), I know something is up. There is nothing wrong with a mom getting away for some girl time, but Jenny's overall persona seems to have changed. As expected, her husband Matt soon reaches out to ask if we can get together and talk. I know exactly what we are going to be discussing: their marriage is in trouble, and he is reaching out for help. We sit down in my office, and, before he opens his mouth, I ask, "Is this about Jenny?" He looks surprised. "How did you know?" I sadly explain that I have seen this several times. Someone gets into "wellness" or health, gets better looking, starts going out with their friends regularly like they were back in college, and before you know it, there are marriage issues. Matt talks me through everything that had started to change in their relationship.

Jenny had become obsessed with wellness, met a few single or divorced girlfriends at her workout class, and the workouts and friends became her entire world. Her friends would stay out late, drinking, laughing, and talking about recent dates they had been on with a lawyer, an accountant, a business owner, etc. One of Jenny's friends had recently separated from her husband and would talk about how free she felt. "I can finally be myself for the first time," she'd told Jenny. Her friend acknowledged that her husband was a great guy and a good dad, but they'd just grown apart.

In light of this new social life, Jenny's own life had begun to look so mundane. She "realized" that with getting married so young, she had never had a chance to discover life and find herself. She went from college, to marriage, to being a mom, and looked back on what seemed like a blur that left her packing lunches every night, driving a minivan, and throwing dinner in the Crock-Pot because her afternoon rush involved picking up various kids from their activities.

Meanwhile, she was harboring resentment that Matt would work his nine-to-five job, play with the kids for a few minutes, and then watch Netflix until he fell asleep around ten. There was nothing exciting about him, but he was her first boyfriend back in college, they fell in love, and this was now it. Like Groundhog Day, the same routine would happen the next morning, and the morning after that, over and over again. Jenny decided it was time to do something for herself, so she got her own apartment and moved out. "You only live once," and Jenny was ready to see if God had something different out there for her, since God "wanted her to follow her heart."

When my wife and I finally get Jenny to sit down and talk, we hear the same story we've heard from dissatisfied spouses time and time again. It's almost like hearing a scripted monologue:

> "I feel like I settled."
> "What if I married the wrong person?"
> "My friends tell me they've never seen me happier since I moved out."
> "I just feel like I need to focus on myself for a while."
> "He's a great guy, and a great dad, but I don't have feelings for him anymore."

And then the famous line: "I believe that God wants me to be happy."

When one thinks of a midlife crisis, we usually think of a man in his mid-fifties buying a convertible, suddenly using a self-tanner, and getting a new hobby. There is a new focus on feeling or looking younger to avoid the reality of aging. When this happens in one's thirties, however, it is about feverishly trying to recover or discover a better version of oneself to avoid the reality of being "regular." The claim is so often that "God wants what is best for me, and it can't be this." There is a deep and visible hunger to which the gospel should be the remedy.

Author and pastor Skye Jethani wrote, "We go online to find a witness to our life . . . what we're really searching for on Facebook, Instagram, and Twitter is someone to tell us, 'You matter. Your life counts.'"[1] The tragedy is that while the Christian life should be the refreshing antidote to this kind of wishful longing, new prosperity churches and influencers are exacerbating it. The world suggests that we solve discontentment or heal from unexpected wounds by pursuing with reckless abandon (and no shame) whatever makes us happy, even if that includes leaving our spouses, having an affair, getting an abortion, cutting out difficult people, etc. And somehow, there are now "Christian" teachers and influencers essentially advocating for the same thing.

In Rachel Hollis's best-selling book, *Girl, Wash Your Face*, she urges readers:

> You are meant to be the hero of your own story.
>
> You, and only you, are ultimately responsible for who you become and how happy you are.
>
> You should be the very first of your priorities.[2]

The book does make scattered references to Jesus, faith, etc. But the teachings are from a totally worldly position, attributing any wisdom in her advice (as Alisa Childers calls out in her review of the book) not to God but to self-love.[3] Childers admits the book, although funny and well-written,

> is littered with references to "self-love" and "self-care." In fact, the theme is so pervasive that it forms the infrastructure for how she responds to everything from hardship to trauma to parenting to working out.
>
> In all of these scenarios, the answer is always something like picking yourself up by your bootstraps and striving and trying and running a marathon and getting therapy. . . . *Anything* but surrendering your life to Jesus and placing your trust in Him.[4]

Jen Oshman reviewed Hollis's follow-up book *Girl, Stop Apologizing*, warning church leaders, "You better believe that Rachel Hollis has forged meaningful relationships with the women in your pews."[5] Oshman points out that *Girl, Wash Your Face* ranked number one on Amazon in Personal Growth and Christianity, as well as Women's Christian Living, for several months. Hollis writes as though she's starting a women's liberation movement, claiming, "All that really matters is how bad you want [your] dreams and what you're willing to do to make them happen."[6] This is an unthinkably un-Christian posture toward "all that really matters." What happens when you aren't as happy as you think you should be? Hollis suggests you just go right ahead and make changes.

Oshman warns against the power of this kind of messaging, given that "in this fallen world, all women are tempted to believe their lives are mediocre and disappointing."[7] Just as Christian men need other Christian men to point them towards their duties in Christ by the power of Christ, Christian women need other sisters in Christ to do the same. Jen Oshman bemoans the kind of advice Rachel Hollis is selling with her massive influence:

On staying home with her kids, Hollis says:

> It's not my spiritual gifting. It's not in my wheelhouse. You know what is in my wheelhouse? Building a successful business, managing a team, writing books, giving keynote speeches, crushing it on social media, strategizing, branding, PR, and planning live events where a thousand women fly in from all over the world to be inspired. (80)

Lest you think I'm passing judgment on Hollis for being a working mom, I assure you that I'm not. I've been a working mom for all of my children's days. But taking up your cross, sacrificially serving others, and staying home with hard, messy, needy children who don't say thank you isn't in *anyone's* wheelhouse. I fear Hollis's instructions will be happily heeded and lead to the emboldened absence of wives, moms, daughters, sisters, and friends who enjoy pursuing their dreams more than loving the least of these.[8]

Childers and Oshman conclude by offering a true remedy, a better way, by pointing to Christ Jesus.[9] Jesus has purchased our freedom and peace, reconciling us to the Father, making us righteous in His sight, and adopting us into God's family as His children. As writer Alisa Childers notes, "If you let this truth become the foundation of how you see the world, you will be content to glorify Him in every situation, whether you're cleaning bathrooms or relaxing at your beach house, changing diapers or crushing your career goals."[10]

Similarly, this line of thinking can overtake men. For example, take Tim, a fictionalized guy:

Lately, home doesn't sound very appealing to Tim anymore. Going out after work for a drink with the office staff went from being an occasional act of bonding with coworkers to a steadily increasing way to avoid the house full of whiny kids and awaiting responsibilities. He especially likes to make sure he goes out for happy hour when his coworker Laura is joining the group. She's recently divorced and around a decade younger than Tim. She is everything that his wife, Natalie, used to be when they first got married, especially before kids. Laura is fun, easygoing, fit, dresses well, and never seems tired like his wife at home. More than that, she laughs at Tim's jokes, respects him at work, and makes him feel confident.

Tim is a churchgoing man and sees his draw to Laura as no more than innocent and fun, nothing out of bounds or inappropriate for a family man like himself. But before long, he's got a pep in his step, someone to impress, and is spending less and less time at home. Tim makes sure he sees the kids but hardly pays much attention to his wife, Natalie. They don't fight or argue; they simply exist in the daily grind as co-parents and roommates.

When Natalie fails to notice the few pounds he's lost, he starts to mention Laura at home, citing her as an example of a fun and outgoing person and a perceptive friend. When his wife gets upset that he neglected to do a household chore she'd been asking about, he gets defensive about how she needs to remember her duty to respect him and that at least when he's at work people don't nag him. Feeling insecure already, Natalie begins to get suspicious that something is going on and shares her fear with Tim, but he lashes out that she's just jealous (or crazy) and that he's allowed to have friends.

His wife is no fool, and sadly, what started as a connection at work is now the relationship that makes Tim feel young and good-looking again, just like back in his college days. His focus on himself and how Laura makes him feel has made him conclude that this must be what God wants for him. Why would God want him home in a marriage he's no longer excited about when he can be with Laura, a girl who makes him feel respected, attractive, and excited? Besides, he concludes, Laura is a good Christian woman, and he can still be an involved dad to his kids, and they will be better off in the long haul with a dad who is happy and fulfilled.

Recently, Tim's been listening to a sermon podcast from a pastor he heard about on social media who says that God never wants people to settle but instead to thrive and experience the destiny God designed for them. Prompted by this newfound "destiny," Tim walks into the room after work one evening and tells his wife he's been praying about this and believes they would be better off just as friends and parents, not husband and wife.

"After all," Tim says, "I think it is what God would want for both of us, and it will allow you to find someone you deserve, too."

I wish I could say these scenarios were far-fetched. But there seems to be an epidemic in my community of people walking away from their marriages, not because they failed to learn the other's love language or didn't balance each other out on their Enneagram, but because the thought of being married to an average man or woman, with average jobs, living in an average house, in an average city, seemed like an unfulfilling and less-than-sufficient life. The life God has given you, and (in the case of marriage and parenthood) has directly called you to, becomes a symbol for all that is keeping you from a "truly" fulfilling life. What started out with butterflies ends up with disdain for being trapped with a nice guy who has a "dad bod" or the woman who has "let herself go."

I know a professing Christian who decided to get divorced because she was about to be forty and claimed there wasn't much window left for her to "get back out there" and find that person who will make her happy. Her husband's crime was being too settled down and living a life that had no adventure. I'm not being snarky; those were her words. Tim Keller, helpful as always, says:

> In the past every culture assumed that you found truth *outside* the self, either in God or tradition or some transcendent values, or in the good of your family and community. That meant we had some objective, external norms by which disputes between persons could be adjudicated. Now our culture says we find truth *inside* ourselves; we are told to "live our truth" and never sacrifice our happiness and inner desires for someone else. To do so is unhealthy at best—oppression at worst. Marriage, however, requires this kind of mutual sacrifice every single day. So it's not surprising that both marriage and also child-bearing is in decline in our culture.[11]

While this is not a chapter on marriage, the effects visible in marriage reveal an underlying problem impacting so many young adults in my city, married or not: in our self-focus, we as a people are chronically discontent. The media inundates us with messaging that we should never have to settle. And instead of being a respite from this chaos, the church is too often laying on more of the same. Contentment is a borderline curse word in pop-Christianity, because not pursuing or desiring something "better" is seen as settling for less than God's best. As if we didn't have enough pressure to measure up to more, now we've got spiritual guilt too?

> **In our self-focus, we as a people are chronically discontent.**

Ironically, the discontented life is one that *is* actually settling for less than God's best. It is the devil who is called the thief, coming to steal, kill, and destroy (see John 10:10). The presence of discontentment in the life of the believer, and convincing us this comes from God-given desires, is part of the strategy he uses to carry out his mission of destruction. Thankfully, there is a much better option for us, as Jesus has life, and has it more abundantly, and this is God's best. The yellow brick road to God's best life for us is one of contentment in Christ, obedience to Christ, fulfillment in Christ. If only we could follow that yellow brick road.

The apostle Paul gives us the map. Writing from prison and facing great hardship, he wrote, "I have learned to be content in whatever circumstances I find myself. I know how to make do with little, and I know how to make do with a lot. In any and all circumstances I have learned the secret of being content—whether well fed or hungry, whether in abundance or in need. I am able to do all things through him who strengthens me" (Phil. 4:11–13).

Pastor Jason Helopoulos notes that Paul both qualifies this as a "secret" and something he has had to learn. That's significant! Helopoulos believes that "discontentment may be the greatest trap in our culture.

> **The yellow brick road to God's best life for us is one of contentment in Christ, obedience to Christ, fulfillment in Christ.**

It may be greater than lust, greed, and even lying, because discontentment leads to all these other sins . . . it feels like the entire world is colluding to stir up discontentment within us. Every billboard, every commercial, every brochure tends to communicate, 'You deserve and need more.'"[12] So how do we learn to abide in the secret Paul discovered? The secret to contentment is a relationship with Jesus Christ. If you are in Christ and you struggle with discontentment, chances are you have not been told, have forgotten, or have failed to believe that you don't have to go around or outside of Christ to find the things you are looking for, such as satisfaction, fulfillment, meaning, purpose, love, belonging, and identity.

If you are pursuing contentment as a Christian, it should mean you are after gospel contentment found in Jesus Christ. Paul makes clear this is non-circumstantial. Paul knows that in Christ he has everything he needs. In Jesus is all. That is why Paul could write earlier in his Philippian letter that for him to live is Christ, and to die is gain (1:21). There is nothing he truly needs for which he must depart from Christ. Yet we so easily believe the lie that there is more to be gained by disobeying God than there is to be gained by obeying Him. This goes back to the first sin in the garden, where Adam and Eve bought into the lie that they were missing out on something better than what God had for them, which (by the way) was a totally unstained, unhindered relationship with Himself. Theirs was the original FOMO (fear of missing out).

When we question God's motives or commands, asking, "Did God really say . . . ?" we're using the language of the devil. This questioning often leads to rationalizing our choices by reaching the conclusion that regardless of what God says, what He really wants is for us to be happy. We put ourselves in the position of God, curating and making judgments about what is and what isn't good for us.

But there is hope in Christ. Part of the journey of Christian discipleship is learning to find Christ to be sufficient. Paul says he can actually do this because of the work of Christ on his behalf. "I am able to do all things through him who strengthens me." On our own, this world is too intoxicating. We can't resist it. We need more. With Jesus, contentment is possible. First and foremost, we have to actually believe that as Christians. We need to know God through His Word. We need Christian fellowship to spur us on. Helopoulos reminds us that we can find all we need in Christ:

> If we desire love, it is found in His spread arms on the cross (Romans 8; Ephesians 3). If we want hope, it is found in his resurrection (1 Corinthians 15:19). If we seek peace, it is found in his blood shed for us (Colossians 1:20). If we seek joy, it is given in His Spirit (Galatians 5). Happiness? It is found in knowing what awaits us (Revelation 21). Power? You will rule with Him forever (Revelation 3:20–21)....
>
> ... [Contentment] is not [in] being self-satisfied or self-fulfilled; it is being Christ-satisfied and Christ-fulfilled.[13]

It truly is all in Christ.

There are times when we have to fight for the right worship. Is it going to be ourselves or Christ who receives our worship? The choices we make in seasons or moments of discontentment determine the answer. By reading the whole of Scripture through the lens in which it was intended—to magnify Christ—we can find guidance on what it is we're to be doing as we practically work out this contentment in Christ. Instead of viewing our families, responsibilities, work, and circumstances as something we're "settling" for, let's have the posture of asking how God would have us submit to Him in worship in those arenas and pour ourselves out for those around us. Submission, not settling. Is it a burden or a blessing to be married? To be a parent? To have coworkers with whom you disagree? How can our lives be places where we rely fully on Christ and pour ourselves out in worshipful submission to Him?

The psalmist wrote, "You reveal the path of life to me; in your presence is abundant joy; at your right hand are eternal pleasures" (Ps. 16:11). Concepts of abundance and pleasure are not outside of God's will; we just have to understand that self-pursuit is not the way to obtain those things and will not deliver

> **How can our lives be places where we rely fully on Christ and pour ourselves out in worshipful submission to Him?**

them in the way we truly desire. He is the source. And He wants His people to live in a state of contentment, knowing that He is the source. Paul reminds us that "godliness with contentment is great gain" (1 Tim. 6:6). Be where you are, working dutifully and joyfully for the Lord, knowing that He's handling the score. Ligon Duncan brings encouragement, reminding us that contentment is not:

innate to Christian experience: It is learned. You don't just trust Jesus and suddenly get content. Oh, yes, there is a certain kind of contentment that comes immediately when we trust in Jesus Christ, but there are battles of contentment to fight all the time, and we don't just become content because we come to Christ. We have to learn contentment. That's encouraging! If you're struggling with contentment, that's incredibly encouraging.[14]

As the song I sang as a teen goes, "All I have in You is more than enough."[15] May that be the song in my head the next time I think there is more to be gained by disobeying God than there is to be gained by obeying Him or that I must go around Him for everything I am looking for in life.

6

Mum's the Word:

Lite on Doctrine and Theology as a Means to Grow the Church

The heart cannot love
what the mind does not know.
—JEN WILKIN

While elements of the new prosperity gospel have been around for a while, I don't think the full-fledged, mainstream movement we're seeing now has been around for long enough to allow for much retrospective analysis. I don't think we've seen the full extent of the damage it is doing. Yet we must be able to consider where it came from and why it has gained traction. I believe the wishy-washy self-help sermons of so many congregations have given rise to a generation of (what I like to call) "atheological" congregants. Unlike an atheist, who holds to the non-existence of God, an atheological person believes in God but doesn't know much doctrine or see that as a problem.

The average churchgoer might not have considered many

issues through the lens of Scripture, either because he or she doesn't think it's necessary or doesn't want to, or because the pastor has never "gone there" during a sermon. This, in turn, has allowed the dynamic and shiny appeal of new prosperity teaching to take flight. Take, for example, the story of David and Goliath. Where moralistic teaching in many churches might have said, "Be a David," new prosperity teaching says, "You ARE a David! You will have the victory over your Goliath." If Christians don't know the Bible, it can be presented to mean whatever the preacher wants it to mean.

I issue this as a warning to all of us, both to individual Christians and especially to pastors and teachers. It's not enough for pastors to have sound theology. We must preach it, lest our people be led astray. Several years ago, I ran into an individual at a coffee shop who had left our church quite some time before. She'd begun a same-sex relationship, and, knowing our church's position on homosexuality, had decided to leave. We believe the Scriptures are clear that God has created sex for a husband and a wife exclusively and that any sex outside of that specific marriage union is sin. We also believe in the grace of God for all people in the redemption of sinners. No person or lifestyle is singled out. (That same message is offensive to those in extramarital heterosexual relationships.) We simply preach the whole counsel of God from the pulpit and in our discipleship environments.

> **Where moralistic teaching in many churches might have said, "Be a David," new prosperity teaching says, "You ARE a David!"**

After a quick hello and some small talk, we started a conversation about her decision to leave our church. I attempted to show grace and understanding in her purpose for leaving.

She certainly would have still been welcome to attend our worship services and small group Bible studies, but I respected the fact that she'd made a principled decision. She knew both parties felt strongly about their views. Then she shared with me where she was now attending church, and I was baffled. "I know that pastor," I said, "and he believes the exact same thing our elders and I do about sexuality. I am absolutely certain of it." She couldn't believe it. In all her time attending her church, she never knew what the pastor of the church believed about such a critical issue. But—please note—this omission led her to believe that he must be supportive, which is why she was comfortable attending.

I called the pastor and gave him a hard time about it. His reason for being silent on homosexuality was simple: he didn't want to offend or have people leave the church. We must consider, though, that not only does our omission of certain truths not make them any less true before God, but also that it is God's unfiltered words through Scripture that bring about true change.

I have been struck by Nehemiah 8 since I was first introduced to the story in a college Bible class. The Israelites had returned from exile and were attempting to rebuild Jerusalem, the Holy City, as they had previously known it. It was a ground zero sort of time for Israel after a long season of humbling and straying from the Lord.

Not only does our omission of certain truths not make them any less true before God, but it is God's unfiltered words through Scripture that bring about true change.

All the people gathered together at the square in front of the Water Gate. They asked the scribe Ezra to bring the book of the law of Moses that the LORD had given Israel. On the first day of the seventh month, the priest Ezra brought the law before the assembly of men, women, and all who could listen with understanding. While he was facing the square in front of the Water Gate, he read out of it from daybreak until noon before the men, the women, and those who could understand. All the people listened attentively to the book of the law. . . . Ezra opened the book in full view of all the people, since he was elevated above everyone. As he opened it, all the people stood up. Ezra blessed the LORD, the great God, and with their hands uplifted all the people said, "Amen, Amen!" Then they knelt low and worshiped the LORD with their faces to the ground. . . .

Nehemiah the governor, Ezra the priest and scribe, and the Levites who were instructing the people said to all of them, "This day is holy to the LORD your God. Do not mourn or weep." For all the people were weeping as they heard the words of the law. Then he said to them, "Go and eat what is rich, drink what is sweet, and send portions to those who have nothing prepared, since today is holy to our Lord. Do not grieve, because the joy of the LORD is your strength." And the Levites quieted all the people, saying, "Be still, since today is holy. Don't grieve." Then all the people began to eat and drink, send portions, and have a great celebration, because they had understood the words that were explained to them.

On the second day, the family heads of all the people, along with the priests and Levites, assembled before the scribe Ezra to study the words of the law. They found written in the law how the LORD had commanded through Moses that the Israelites should dwell in shelters during the festival of the seventh month. So they proclaimed and spread this news throughout their towns and in Jerusalem, saying, "Go out to the hill country and bring back branches of olive, wild olive, myrtle, palm, and other leafy trees to make shelters, just as it is written." The people went out, brought back branches, and made shelters for themselves on each of their rooftops and courtyards, the court of the house of God, the square by the Water Gate, and the square by the Ephraim Gate. The whole community that had returned from exile made shelters and lived in them. The Israelites had not celebrated like this from the days of Joshua son of Nun until that day. And there was tremendous joy. Ezra read out of the book of the law of God every day, from the first day to the last. The Israelites celebrated the festival for seven days, and on the eighth day there was a solemn assembly, according to the ordinance. (Neh. 8:1–18, selected)

This story stunned me. A crowd gathered, asked for God's Word, and stood to hear it. Upon hearing it, they fell to their feet worshiping and weeping. They were made aware of their short-comings before God, and, coming into compliance with the Word (most immediately through observing the festival that happened to fall on the time of year of their corporate reading), their collective joy "was very great." The Word was the experience. It wasn't a key change, inspirational story, powerful video, or testimony that brought them to their feet in reverence, and then to their knees in worship. It was the reading of the Scriptures. What is it today that produces worship corporately in us? And how long has it been since some of us have felt that sweet fullness of "experiencing" God through His Word?

A pastor of a new prosperity church once told me, "My theology is just to love Jesus." While this sounds like a noble mindset, it is par for the course in pop-Christianity, where it is hard to discern what the pastor actually believes about the Jesus he claims to love. It is rare to know where a pop-Christian pastor stands concerning many areas of doctrine, because (in the spirit of pragmatism and popularity) he simply doesn't believe it is necessary.

We see this outside the sermons as well. Take, for example, music used in a worship service. Many of the popular songs are vague, repetitive, devoid of anything too specific. Traditional, historical hymns are seen as archaic, too wordy, not relevant. And let's not even talk about artists who sing the Psalms exactly as written; those won't get sung in most modern churches. "If you really want to engage people," writes Aaron Armstrong, "you need to infuse your worship with sound doctrine."[1] Quoting Bobby Jamieson, Armstrong emphasizes, "Sound doctrine teaches us to delight in God because it shows us how delightful God is. . . . It holds before our eyes the perfections of his character, the abundance of his grace, and the majesty of his sovereign rule over all things."[2]

> It wasn't a key change, inspirational story, powerful video, or testimony that brought them to their feet in reverence, and then to their knees in worship. It was the reading of the Scriptures.

Our musical worship should not be atheological, and it should not be the case that "puffy, fluffy songs that could as easily be about a girlfriend or boyfriend as about Jesus dominate the worship 'set.'"[3] The songs chosen for a Sunday morning service should be part of the overall goal to teach about Christ and encourage the congregation in the truth—not "to 'facilitate' (read:

'manufacture') an intense emotional experience.... Emotions are good things, but creating emotional experiences flips the object of the worship gathering from God to us."[4]

It's been said that songs are "the theology people remember." Imagine how richly you could equip your congregation (or, to the individual reader, your own heart and mind) with actual, foundational truths about God? How much more comforting in times of trial are biblical promises about God's character than vapid statements about a generic sort of feeling? Our worship should be in response to something, and if it isn't the truths of God's Word, then what exactly is it? Armstrong says that if we are going to figuratively "lose ourselves in worship," we're to "lose ourselves in awe of the God who is, who has called us to himself, and who saves and sanctifies us through his Word."[5]

Scott Swain writes that biblical doctrine "taught by the Father through the son in the Holy Spirit, informs our faith and guides our love."[6] We must know what the Bible says in order to really believe it. We must center our entire lives and worldviews on the teachings of the Bible. While our salvation is by faith alone through grace, doctrine is a key mechanism by which we can know and love God.

> **How much more comforting in times of trial are biblical promises about God's character than vapid statements about a generic sort of feeling?**

You can be legally married to someone, but if you don't seek to know anything about your spouse, it can hardly be argued that you love them. This is why Paul instructed Timothy to "hold on to the pattern of sound teaching that you have heard from me, in the faith and love that are in Christ Jesus" (2 Tim. 1:13). Doctrine is critical to our spiritual health. Swain adds that "Christian doctrine has a twofold object. The primary object of doctrine is God; the secondary object is all things in relation to God. Doctrine teaches us to see God as the one from whom and through whom and to whom all things exist, and doctrine directs our lives to this God's glory (Rom. 11:36; 1 Cor. 8:6)."

If we're not careful, we can perpetuate what atheological preaching and discipleship have produced: a generation of believers who don't think doctrine is a very big deal. That is a slippery slope to a following generation with no sort of convictions whatsoever. A friend of mine sat down for lunch with a staff member from a large new prosperity gospel church. They covered a wide range of topics and somehow got on the topic of conflict at my friend's former church over whether it was essential to believe in the virgin birth of Christ. The new prosperity church staff member shrugged it off as not a huge deal and said, "I don't think we should get caught up in all that in our churches. Let's just love God, love others, and see people come together. That's what God wants." I truly don't think this man knew any better, and my spirit and tone are not patronizing as I claim this. He has been taught that loving God, loving others, and church unity matter more than whether Jesus was born of a virgin.

While not all doctrinal principles or views could be covered in this book, I want to use the virgin birth as an example to demonstrate why doctrine does matter. Many things ride on the virgin birth that would greatly impact our love of God, others, and the unity of the church should it not be true. John Frame outlines some reasons:

(1) The doctrine of Scripture. If Scripture errs here, then why should we trust its claims about other supernatural

events, such as the resurrection? (2) The deity of Christ. While we cannot say dogmatically that God could enter the world only through a virgin birth, surely the incarnation is a supernatural event if it is anything. To eliminate the supernatural from this event is inevitably to compromise the divine dimension of it. (3) The humanity of Christ. . . . Jesus was *really* born; he *really* became one of us. (4) The sinlessness of Christ. If he were born of two human parents, it is very difficult to conceive how he could have been exempted from the guilt of Adam's sin and become a new head to the human race. . . . Jesus' sinlessness as the new head of the human race and as the atoning lamb of God is absolutely vital to our salvation (2 Cor. 5:21; 1 Pet. 2:22–24; Heb. 4:15; 7:26; Rom. 5:18–19). (5) The nature of grace. The birth of Christ, in which the initiative and power are all of God, is an apt picture of God's saving grace in general of which it is a part. It teaches us that salvation is by God's act, not our human effort.[7]

To distill that, the point I'm trying to make is that there's a very short bridge between a single doctrine not seeming relevant and the entire Bible not seeming relevant. And then what are we even doing? I am not asking every believer to have a PhD in Christology, but I'm hoping that a church staffer who desires to love God, love others, and seek unity would love God by caring about what His Word says, love others by presenting Jesus as is portrayed by the Scriptures, and want a church unity that is not generic but founded upon the Word of God.

It sounds nice to be indifferent toward doctrine in the favor of what appears noble, but not when the entire foundation of the faith hangs on doctrine. I believe the motives are pure for many members of new prosperity churches not wanting to worry about matters of doctrine and theology. But I believe that's a misguided omission. We must be able to develop and strengthen our filters and discernment in order to know what is of God and what isn't. And I'm not even talking about the countless commentaries and books written about doctrine. I'm talking about what's in the Bible itself.

Jesus prayed for unity in John chapter 17. "Sanctify them by the truth; your word is truth. As you sent me into the world, I also have sent them into the world. I sanctify myself for them, so that they also may be sanctified by the truth. . . . May they all be one, as you, Father, are in me and I am in you" (John 17:17–19, 21). Church unity isn't vague. It must be based on truth. Those who depart from orthodoxy are the ones who bring about disunity. To preserve biblical unity is to maintain orthodoxy. There is a desperate need for more Christ-centered, doctrinal, theological preaching and teaching. In the new prosperity church, it simply isn't happening. Author Bryan Litfin, writing about Augustine, said, "[Augustine] had the wisdom to discern sound doctrine, the courage to defend it, and the pastoral love to demand it from his people."[8] It is easy to assume that one who stresses the importance of doctrine perhaps makes little of the practical teachings of the Bible, but it is doctrine that leads Christians to practice. Writing about his study of Francis Turretin's *Institutes of Elenctic Theology*, where he works through the faux rivalry between the theoretical and the practical, Kevin DeYoung recaps:

> Is theology theoretical or practical? From our vantage point, the answer seems obvious. Theology must be practical. It must result in faith and obedience. It must bear fruit. The great problem in our day, we think, is that so much of our

theological discourse has become theoretical–speculative, esoteric, good for nothing but puffing up smart guys with big brains.

But Turretin argues that theology cannot be simply one or the other. True theology is "mixed," partly theoretical and partly practical.[9]

Turretin wrote, "A practical system is that which does not consist in the knowledge of a thing alone, but in its very nature and by itself goes forth into practice and has operation for its object."[10] In other words, right doctrine must mean something in our lives. Theology is extremely practical, because the knowledge of God and His Word drives the outworking of it in our lives, by the Spirit. DeYoung points out that "Turretin insisted that knowledge of God and worship of God could not be separated, just like knowing what is right and doing what is right must be held together."[11] It is important to note, however, that a sermon doesn't have to give application points for one's daily life in order to be biblical and practical. Pointing one to the greatness, glory, and love of Christ is certainly practical and the most important takeaway from a sermon one can ever receive.

7

All Hat, No Cattle:

The False Advertisement of New Prosperity Churches

It very often happens that the converts that are born
in excitement die when the excitement is over.
—CHARLES SPURGEON

"Well, we are 10-0! What's not to be excited about?" I asked my
friend Joe after he was skeptical of our favorite college football
team. I thought he was crazy. How can you be skeptical about a
team who is ranked second in the nation with one week to go?

"Winning can cover a lot of holes and flaws," he replied with
certainty. Sure, our team had squeaked by against some pretty bad
teams several times that season, but who cares, we were 10-0!

Well, what do you know, we lost the last game of the season,
then lost by more than forty points in the conference champion-
ship game, and then lost the bowl game. The next season, the team
went 6-6. There was a bad offensive line, average wide receivers,
and a quarterback who was pretty rough. Joe was right. Those

miracle wins had covered up the reality that this team had problems. Eventually, they were exposed.

When one looks at new prosperity churches, at first glance it is hard to see why anyone would have an issue or be concerned. People are coming. Lots of them. Especially young adults, which we're tempted to assume is a wonderful thing. With all the data we see about young people leaving churches in droves, shouldn't we celebrate what is happening in these churches? But crowds can be misleading. Just reconsider the large crowd Jesus fed with loaves and fish. They were all-in as their needs were being met and hit the road when the big spectacle was over. It's not that Jesus wasn't a successful or engaging speaker; it's that when push came to shove, the crowd was there for the wrong reasons. And let's be honest— no other leader is Jesus. Just because something appears to be successful doesn't mean it is legitimate. Like my 10-0 football team, it could be a house of cards. Jesus tells us where to put our stock:

> "Therefore, everyone who hears these words of mine and acts on them will be like a wise man who built his house on the rock. The rain fell, the rivers rose, and the winds blew and pounded that house. Yet it didn't collapse, because its foundation was on the rock. But everyone who hears these words of mine and doesn't act on them will be like a foolish man who built his house on the sand. The rain fell, the rivers rose, the winds blew and pounded that house, and it collapsed. It collapsed with a great crash." (Matt. 7:24–27)

Notice that the house on the sand was actually built. It was a freestanding, seemingly viable structure. Perhaps it even had a waterfront view and tons of great Airbnb reviews. But the foundation was poor and when trouble came, it couldn't hold up. As the old Texas saying goes, it was all hat and no cattle.

As a younger pastor, I used to get annoyed when someone would throw out the critique "What you win them with, you win them to." It appeared to me to be an attack on a style of worship service people didn't prefer. Somehow a worship service with a three hundred-person choir, top-shelf orchestra, and soloists was a powerful expression of worship, but a guitar solo was considered showy, shallow, and entertainment-driven. I'd hear "What you win them with is what you win them to," and I'd roll my eyes. If the Scriptures are rightly preached and the gospel message made clear, I don't care if a worship service has a band, a choir, a pastor in a robe, or a guy in jeans. I still feel like this critique can be used unnecessarily when focusing on style or tertiary issues of preference. But as I've matured, I have a greater understanding of when it should be used: to test preaching, theology, and the actual draw and focus of a church.

If you reach people *with* a God-and-country message, you will reach them to a God-and-country message, believing that nationalism is a Christian virtue and political victories a mission of the church.

If you reach people *with* a social gospel, you will reach them to a social gospel, believing that humanitarian work, even if devoid of gospel proclamation, is the true mission of the church.

If you reach people *with* legalism, you will reach people to legalism, believing their moral performance is part of what makes them right with God. As a result, they will look down on others who don't measure up to their cultural standards of rule-following.

And herein lies a great concern regarding the success of new prosperity gospel churches. What you win them with, you win them to. The message matters. The emphasis matters. The focus matters. We must not be selling real estate in pits of sand and giving our congregants building materials. We must point them to the rock. In 2007, Mark Galli wrote about his concern over the marketing movement of churches, believing there is a reason Jesus said, "You shall be my witnesses," and not "You shall be my marketers." Galli asks:

> Should it surprise us that in this church-marketing era, members demand more and more from their churches, and if churches don't deliver, they take their spiritual business elsewhere? Have we ever seen an age in which church transience was such an epidemic? [1]

Galli continues:

> Should it surprise us that in this era, pastors increasingly think of themselves as "managers," "leaders," and "CEOs" of "dynamic and growing congregations," rather than as shepherds, teachers, and servants of people who need to know God? .... Today churches large and small (the small imitating the large) have unthinkingly adopted a marketing mentality that, it turns out, subverts rather than promotes the gospel.[2]

What you win them with is what you win them to.

Commenting on Galli's piece, Jared C. Wilson adds, "What was once idealized as 'church can be the place where one experiences spiritual truth' has become 'church is the place where a spiritual product can be consumed.'"[3] Jared doesn't pull any punches concerning these churches, claiming, "You'd think Jesus and the disciples were playing clips from Sophocles, punctuated by some powerful ballad with Peter on the lute, and then a tidy little message on how to succeed as a fisherman."[4]

What Is Your Church Selling?

> We must not be selling real estate in pits of sand and giving our congregants building materials. We must point them to the rock.

Have you ever noticed that the more fervently someone on social media is trying to convince you that they're killing it, the easier it is to see that they're not? Church should be a place where one's soul is refreshed and filled, but not with vague self-care, self-help mantras set to the backdrop of the Old Testament and culminating in the victory essential oil of the blood of Jesus. Pastor John Starke reminds us that self-care "can be important. But let's be aware that the self-care industry aims us towards 'optimized' lives rather than renewal. It's something you perform, post, and share. It's one more performative way you display to the world that you're *okay.*"[5] Watching the subculture of the new prosperity gospel appear through selfies and inspirational quotes of friends and acquaintances makes me wonder if these friends ever get exhausted from everything always having to be a 10/10.

In his book, *Gentle and Lowly*, Dane Ortlund wrote:

> There is an entire psychological substructure that, due to the fall, is a near-constant manufacturing of relational leveraging, fear-stuffing, nervousness, score-keeping, neurotic-controlling, anxiety-festering silliness that is not something we say or even think so much as something we exhale. You can smell it on people, though some of us are good at hiding it. And if you trace this fountain of scurrying

haste, in all its various manifestations, down to the root, you don't find childhood difficulties or a Myers-Briggs diagnosis or Freudian impulses. You find gospel deficit. You find lack of felt awareness of Christ's heart. All the worry and dysfunction and resentment are the natural fruit of living in a mental universe of law. The felt love of Christ really is what brings rest, wholeness, flourishing, shalom.[6]

Disciples of the new prosperity gospel are seeking something experiential and lasting, but we must realize that they don't need to go around the gospel to find what they are looking for in their lives. God's love, in Christ, is the experience. The help we need is not a "better" version of the self, but a more God-glorifying, self-denying, raised-from-the-dead self. We are fooling ourselves if we think gospel-centrality isn't enough of a "hook" to keep our churches viable.

We must not, like so many churches compromising or fully neglecting the gospel, allow our primary concerns to be drawing people in with the music, the lighting, the personalities of the people on stage. Because "the function of the pulpit is not to entertain, to amuse, to satisfy an idle curiosity: it is to . . . keep ever before men the one supreme figure in history, the Lord Jesus Christ, and to beget within them a passion for him, and for a Christly life."[7] How do you keep the person and work of Christ in front of people as the primary focus when soothing self-help messaging and emotional experiences are center stage? What you win them with, you win

> **The help we need is not a "better" version of the self, but a more God-glorifying, self-denying, raised-from-the-dead self.**

them to. Tony Robbins and Oprah Winfrey draw big crowds too. All hat, no gospel cattle; all bait, no gospel switch.

What Is Your Church Showcasing?

"Excellence" is a preeminent focus in a new prosperity worship service. Rightly, its proponents would likely point to principles from Scripture, such as "working as unto the Lord" or "giving God your firstfruits," but the definition of excellence here seems to be more about a style than about pursuing Christian virtue, justifying extravagance and a production value that would intrigue a Super Bowl halftime show planning committee. While I personally prefer a modern style and appreciate churches attempting to make things run smoothly during a service, I worry that using the word "excellence" in the context of style and production seems to be reserved for only certain kinds and styles of churches. These services have high standards and attract only the prettiest, most talented, and trendiest people to the platform, all in the name of giving God their best. Yet excellence, in a Christian understanding, is about heart and noble effort more than product and skill. Colossians 3:23 calls us, "Whatever you do, do it from the heart, as something done for the Lord and not for people."

I'm afraid that, too often, the pressure to be amazing or to seem amazing is not done for God, but rather for people. It scares me a bit how much we have co-opted services intended for the worship of a holy and terrifying God. It worries me that "excellence" has become a justification for rewarding the best and brightest, making them not servants of the congregation, but VIPs and professional green room occupants. And further, it casts a shadow on churches that simply aren't able to pull off high production as though they aren't committed to excellence.

In an article, Jared C. Wilson tells of the backlash he once got for posting: "At our church we want our music to be as good as it can be without having people come to our church because of it."[8] I can imagine many an angry Twitter troll implying that he hates "good music" and wanted to vilify the arts. Don't get me wrong; I love church music. I love the music at the church where I pastor. I also prefer good stage lighting and rock bands as my style of choice for a Sunday morning. But I absolutely believe that singing the Word together as a congregation is the point. It is not a concert. Something different has happened in pop-Christianity that has turned music into more than congregational singing. It is now an experience with higher expectations than the quality and content of the sermon. Depending on the size and budget of the church, it is a quasi-celebrity driven, must-see event. And smaller churches seek to emulate this status.

Author Mike Cosper writes, "Celebrity culture turns pastors and worship leaders into icons. Celebrity culture turns worship gatherings into rock concerts. Celebrity culture confuses flash and hype for substance."[9] These services, Cosper adds, are an "emotional ride led by a hip, handsome, and passionate rock star." The music is followed by a "communicator" whose message, as Aaron Armstrong wrote, "seems to be less about what Jesus has done for you and is doing in you, and more about what you are doing to unlock, release, and call down God's blessing and realize your life potential."[10]

Cosper asks whether the church is a gathering and sending of saints or a rally for a fan club.[11] If forced to pick, I wonder how many Christians would choose experiential, stylistic preferences over the substance of what is sung and taught by their church. Actually, some have already made that decision based on the churches they're attending. I believe there are many important elements of a church gathering, but the faithful preaching of God's Word should be supreme.

I want to win people with a message that would still apply if my church was in a third world country, meeting in secret with nothing more than a single, shared Bible: the message of Jesus Christ crucified, risen, and ascended. Because what you win them with, you win them to.

8

Context Is King:

How Selective Bible Verses Fuel the Movement

"You're so vain, you probably think
this song is about you."
—CARLY SIMON

In popular American Christianity, it is common to believe that the whole Bible is about us. We either read ourselves into Bible stories that might be exclusively descriptive of a historic event that has already taken place, or we take a verse completely out of context to claim it as a promise for something unrelated to the original meaning. This method, employed by new prosperity preachers, has been referred to by critics as "narcigesis." (The technical term for interpreting meaning from Scripture is "exegesis.") In the narcigesis method, you take a passage of Scripture and completely center it on yourself or your listeners.

This is not always caused by malicious intent, especially because we're so often conditioned to ask, "What truth, commands, or promises can I take and apply to my own life?" But we must begin with the foundational understanding that the storyline of the Bible is about God and His glory. His greatness is the centerpiece of Scripture, ultimately understood in the redemption of sinners through the death, resurrection, and second coming of Christ. Christopher Wright, in his book about God's mission as portrayed in Scripture, writes, "We ask, 'Where does God fit into the story of my life?' when the real question is where does my little life fit into this great story of God's mission."[1] It is not a minor issue to miss the point of the Bible altogether, let alone to make it about ourselves.

The Bible says about itself that it is "profitable for teaching, for rebuking, for correcting, for training in righteousness, so that the man of God may be complete, equipped for every good work" (2 Tim. 3:16–17). It is certainly the book that applies to our lives more than any other book. Without question, it is more relevant to us than anything else on the planet. It is full of good news for us, wonderful promises for us, and encouraging, soul-reviving truth for us. But it is also God's revelation of Himself, His great salvation, and instructions on how to now live a life that honors Him on His mission. (And, as we'll soon discuss, God's mission does involve wonderful and fulfilling things for us, since Christ Himself is the gift.) Our problem is when we're trying to use Christianity to be a better version of ourselves rather than a more accurate reflection of Him. That is how self-actualization invades our understanding of the Bible.

It is difficult to get over yourself when your primary focus is on God's promises of prosperity more than the promise of Christ. Narcigesis comes alive through the preaching of isolated texts to derive a completely new meaning out of a Bible story to fit your circumstances. Consider this quote from a prominent pastor, who apparently believes the stone being rolled away on Easter morning is an allegory for us to overcome setbacks: "You think it's been too long; it didn't happen in time. So you put the stone over the promise, put the stone over the dream. But you have to do your part and roll that stone away. Start believing again. Get your passion back."[2] I have absolutely no idea how you get there from the story of the resurrection, but people eat it up. Somehow Easter is about your personal dreams. Worse than that, perhaps, the responsibility is on you to roll away the stone.

While it's common to hear sermons about being a David, or being a Peter walking on the water, I want to highlight three popular verses that, when used improperly, tickle the ears of hearers and fuel a me-centered Christianity. They show up on coffee mugs, iPhone lock screens, and are especially loved by young and ambitious Christians. These are the Big 3 of New Prosperity:

1. Psalm 37:4

Take delight in the LORD,
and he will give you your heart's desires.

Wow, we think. *If I want to land that big internship in New York City, I just need to delight in God and He will make my greatest dreams come true.* Speaking of the Christian conversion experience, Nancy Guthrie notes, "When we come to Christ, I think that we expect that God is going to change how we think and that being joined to Christ is going to change how we behave. I think we don't always anticipate that being joined to Christ is going to change how we feel and even what we want."[3] It's not that He gives us what we desire; He actually gives us new desires so that we find ourselves wanting more of Him, and what He has for us, making us more like Jesus.

I have counseled individuals who have had a crisis of faith because they believed they were doing their best to delight in the Lord and were still not getting what they wanted. As we grow in our faith, God gives us His desires for us, which only become clear when we read His Word (in context!) and receive what He has spoken to us through the Scriptures. Reading snippets in isolation or hearing them preached out of context is not going to yield the same result. Psalm 37:4 is certainly about us, but it is about our ongoing transformation to want what God wants for us, our alignment with His Word, mission, and glory. Reading even just that one psalm in its entirety, you'll notice numerous references to committing our steps to God, waiting for God to move, living righteously, depending on God's deliverance, etc. The psalmist is drawing comparisons between the righteous and the wicked—those holistically given to God and those given to themselves. It's clear in the psalm that the wicked don't get to be benefactors of verse four.

So we've covered the "He will give us" part. And what are we to think of desires themselves? First John states that "everything in the world—the lust of the flesh, the lust of the eyes, and the pride in one's possessions—is not from the Father, but is from the world" (1 John 2:16). Concerning this verse, biblical counselor David Powlison wrote, "the term 'lust' has become almost useless to modern readers of the Bible. It is reduced to sexual desire. Take a poll of the people in your church, asking them the meaning of 'lusts of the flesh.'

> It's not that God gives us what we desire; He actually gives us new desires so that we find ourselves wanting more of Him, and what He has for us, making us more like Jesus.

Sex will appear on every list. Greed, pride, gluttonous craving, or mammon worship might be added in the answers of a few of the more thoughtful believers."[4] But we must acknowledge that lust is a desire for anything other than God. It's not enough to avoid sexual lust. We must also not give ourselves to desire for "money, reputation, success, looks, and love."[5]

After one's conversion to Christ there will be a struggle between what God wants and what we want. In the new prosperity gospel, the unofficial solution to this inner battle is to make God switch His position to your side and make Him an advocate of your personal self-fulfillment. Psalm 37:4 is viewed as proof that this is what God intends. But considering the whole of Scripture, we know this is not the case. Instead, let's interpret Psalm 37:4 by first considering who we know God to be: concerned with the glory of His name and the holiness of His people. He is looking out for His people, and so many of our earthly desires will not satisfy. What if we consider that He will give us *Himself* and thereby give us all that we truly desire? "And the world with its lust is passing away, but the one who does the will of God remains forever" (1 John 2:17). Why settle for anything less than God's actual best?

2. Jeremiah 29:11

"For I know the plans I have for you"—this is the LORD's declaration— "plans for your well-being, not for disaster, to give you a future and a hope."

This could be considered the theme verse of American popular Christianity. If the prophet Jeremiah could receive royalties from the amount of times this verse is used during high school graduation season, he would make Jeff Bezos and Mark Zuckerberg look like college students living off Ramen noodles. I see people posting this verse on social media who haven't been to church since their first communion, and I even know a self-professing "spiritual, but not religious" person who has the verse reference tattooed on his bicep. At face value, it's not hard to see how people interpret this verse to mean that "God has a plan for me, and it is good." I definitely believe that God has a plan for us. What would be the point of life if He didn't? But we must understand Jeremiah 29:11 in its proper context so we don't read a Dr. Seuss *Oh-The-Places-You'll-Go* flavor into the Bible.

As Russell Moore summarizes, "the Book of Jeremiah is all about God disrupting his people's plans and upending his people's dreams."[6] That doesn't sound like something I want to have on my coffee mug. Concerning the placement of 29:11 in the larger book, Moore explains that at this point in history, God's people were scattered in captivity. Some remained in Jerusalem and assumed this was a sign of God's favor, while those taken to Babylon were tempted to view themselves as written out of His favor. But the prophet Jeremiah had shocking news for both groups: that "God's judgment [would] fall on Jerusalem, and that God's purposes [would] spring to life through the exiles . . . [but that] their return from exile [wouldn't] happen anytime in their generation, so they should create new lives in Babylon."[7]

So much for exciting plans! God had a plan in Jeremiah 29, but it seemed to be the letdown of a lifetime unless we understand the big picture of the Scriptures—the storyline of God's redemption of His people and of all creation. His plans to bring us good and not harm culminate in Jesus Christ, not in the American Dream. God's plan for us in Christ still stands today as we find ourselves as "strangers and exiles" (1 Peter 2:11) in this life. Part of that plan is that "he who started a good work in you will carry it on to completion until the day of Christ Jesus" (Phil. 1:6). Moore says we can know God's plan for us—you can know God's plan for your life—"the way the exiles of old did: not by observing our present condition but by the word of God, His oath and His covenant. That means that our plans may evaporate. Our dreams may be crushed. Our lives might be snuffed out. But the God who raised Jesus from the dead will raise us up with him."[8] I can't think of a better and more comforting truth to share with a high school graduate who knows Jesus. Jeremiah 29:11 has something far better for you than anything this world has to offer. It has Jesus and redemption in Him, despite the circumstances.

> **His plans to bring us good and not harm culminate in Jesus Christ, not in the American Dream.**

3. Romans 8:31

What, then, are we to say about these things? If God is for us, who is against us?

This is my personal favorite Bible verse. Not because it means that I can take on the world and finish the goals and tasks in front of me, but because of what it says about the results of God's love understood in our salvation. Romans 8:31 is a summary of everything Paul had communicated to the readers in Romans 5–8. Because of our justification by the death and resurrection of Jesus Christ:

We have peace with God. (5:1)
We are reconciled to Him. (5:10–11)

We are saved from wrath. (5:9)

We have the gift of righteousness. (5:17)

We have eternal life. (5:21)

We are dead to sin (6:11) and set free from it. (6:18)

We are alive to God. (6:11)

We are under grace. (6:14)

There is now no condemnation for us. (8:1)

How are we to process all of this? It's almost as if Paul reaches the crescendo of the argument, exhales in relief and joy, and then asks the only logical question, "What then shall we say to these things? If God is for us, who can be against us?" It seems like he could be speechless. But the power of these verses isn't in a key change during a worship song; it's in the truth that God is for us. Think of all that Paul had endured during his apostleship for Christ. Persecution, imprisonment, being shipwrecked, etc. Before then, being someone who persecuted and advocated for the murder of Christians! In the gospel, God is for that man.

Paul carries out the implications of this amazing reality by reminding the church that nobody can bring a charge against God's people (8:33), and they are not under any condemnation, since Jesus became condemned in their place. Now nothing can separate them from God's love (8:34–39). How much better is this true meaning of God being "for us" than the twisted meaning that He is for our personal advancement or success?

While I want to be cautious here, since I believe many congregants of prosperity churches mean well, it is important to remember that pastors, preachers, and teachers have an increased responsibility before the Lord (James 3:1). Thus I would assert that those who teach a gospel centered on man are either false teachers, intentionally distorting the truth, or have not done enough study of their own to grasp the content of the full canon of Scripture. Read enough of the Bible in context, and you'll find something that offends you. I guarantee it. I challenge every Christian to consider the worldly beliefs lingering in our hearts and prayerfully ask God to reveal what in our theology is self-centric instead of Christ-centric, especially if we have a handful of memorized verses that bolster our me-centered faith.

9

Sharing the Spotlight:

Pursuing Greater Things for Ourselves "in Jesus' Name"

"Truly I tell you, the one who believes in me
will also do the works that I do.
And he will do even greater works than these."
—JOHN 14:12

What an amazing statement from Jesus. We will do greater works than Jesus did? What does that mean? "Greater" things sound wonderful. One well-known pastor even wrote a book entitled *Greater*. The official website of the book urges, "If you're tired of being ordinary, it's time to dream bigger. . . . It's time to ignite God's greater vision for your life."[1] The book certainly and rightly points to God as the source of strength for our lives. But the focus of the message is achieving what you've always dreamed of and not living an ordinary life. It all goes back, once again, to the individual and to desiring something more. It rests upon me "unlocking" some next level of faith to get new prizes. Personally, I do hope every Christian desires to know God's vision for their life, because, thankfully, He doesn't leave us hanging on what it is. Scripture is clear: God's vision for our lives is for us to lose ourselves in service to Him and to become more like Jesus by His power. Jesus told His disciples, "If anyone wants to follow after me, let him deny himself, take up his cross daily, and follow me. For whoever wants to save his life will lose it, but whoever loses his life because of me will save it" (Luke 9:23–24).

"Take Up His Cross . . . "

Jesus is calling His disciples to attend a daily funeral for their own ambitions and pride. The cross was not a piece of jewelry in New Testament times. It wasn't a living room decoration carved nicely to fit on the mantel. There weren't crosses hanging in any place of worship. A cross meant one thing: death. It was a curse to hang on one, to receive capital punishment in a gruesome manner for crimes committed. It would be the equivalent of being told to pick up your lethal injection or electric chair. For Jesus to tell His followers to carry their crosses (prior to His own death, which would probably have shed light on the metaphor) meant a call to die to themselves. This probably sounded insane, but is much better than the alternative given in the next verse: "For what does it benefit someone if he gains the whole world, and yet loses or forfeits himself?" (Luke 9:25).

This is hard for those of us living in twenty-first-century America to grasp, as denying ourselves is often reduced to trivial inconveniences or allowing someone else to pick the restaurant we go to after church. But our Christian brothers and sisters in the early church sometimes faced an imminent martyr's death or complete expulsion from their families due to the decision to give their allegiance to Jesus Christ. We have Christian brothers and sisters around the globe now who experience those costs of following Christ. The "greater things" Jesus promised were not going to come with an earthly crown, decorated with the jewels of their God-sized dreams. They were going to come with a cross, ultimately the cross of their Lord, who would give His life so they could inherit a different kingdom than this world—one that is eternal, yet to come.

The new prosperity gospel positions us as the primary actors and securers of our blessing if we "activate" our faith in victory. Yet we know the Bible clarifies that Jesus is the author and perfecter of our faith (Heb. 12:2) and that God is carrying on to completion the good work He started in us (Phil. 1:6). Our God did all the work in saving us, and He decides who we are to be. John the Baptist modeled the proper posture when confronted about his ministry's dwindling popularity as Jesus' earthly ministry picked up speed, saying that "[Jesus] must increase, but I must decrease" (John 3:30). How we are to serve in the grand scheme of history is not ours to determine. Matt Fuller pointed out that "the great irony is that if we exchange the glorious humility that the Lord has given us for an insignificant self-importance, we become far less."[2] In the desire for something greater, it is easy to miss that the actual road to the greater things Jesus promised is not paved with our desires but with small steps of obedience and faithfulness as soldiers in His kingdom and mission.

I draw heavily from D. A. Carson's writings on what Jesus meant by "greater things" in John 14, as well as some advice he gives when young, zealous Christians ask how they should "leverage" their gifts for maximum kingdom impact. On John 14, Carson writes:

> [The disciples] are privileged to participate in the effects of Jesus's completed work. Until he returned to his Father and

bestowed the Holy Spirit, everything Jesus did was of necessity still incomplete. By contrast, the works of the disciples participate in the new situation that exists once Jesus's work is complete. Their works are greater in that they are privileged to take place after the moment of fulfillment.[3]

Getting to participate in this mission and live in this completed work of Christ is far greater than anything else I can imagine this side of heaven. It is a tremendously rich blessing that Jesus says we get to be part of this together. Carson explains:

Jesus's departure through death and resurrection to exaltation is the precondition of his disciples' mission. Because he "goes to the Father," the church embarks on her mission. Moreover, Jesus's exaltation is the precondition of the descent of the promised Holy Spirit (John 7:39; 16:7), who will work with the disciples in their witness (John 15:26; cf. 16:7–11). For these reasons, the followers of Jesus will perform "greater" works.[4]

In pop-Christian circles, doing greater things simply means greater success or a greater spotlight. Even more conservative believers may frame this under the notion that they want to make greater impact for the kingdom. Whether you're claiming "the best is yet to come" or "I want to use my gifts for God's glory on the biggest platform possible," this is a dangerous lust and one Christians must be willing to quickly recognize in themselves. Carson gives guidance:

While most of us go through life afraid that people will think too little of us, one cannot help but notice that Paul goes

through life afraid that people will think too much of him
(2 Cor 12:6). If you grow in your knowledge of sin and of
your own heart, and of the matchless grace in the cross, your
fear will increasingly run in the same direction as Paul's—
and then so-called "spotlight" ministry will increasingly
become something you fear more than lust after.[5]

I believe I can learn something from Christians in the pop-
Christianity realm when it comes to having faith that God can
truly do great things and that He answers prayer. I appreciate that
posture. I desire for my faith to be large. In fact, I want it to be
greater. But I want it to be a biblical one, where there is less of
me and more of God. I need Christian discipleship reminding
me of that goal and not reinforcing my natural human inclination
to want to make much of myself. Carson asks, "Why is it that so
few ostensible prophecies tell people today how much they must
suffer for Jesus's sake?"[6] He notes that after the Damascus Road
experience, God tells Paul not how influential he will be but how
much he must suffer for the mis-
sion to which he's been called.
Charles Spurgeon wrote about
a haunting experience wrestling
with his own ambition, saying it
was as if he heard a voice behind
him saying, "Seekest thou great
things for thyself? Seek them
not; seek them not."[7]

In new prosperity gospel
environments, it is common to
see the church "equipping" someone not by prepping them for
spiritual hardship and solidifying their understanding of the

> **I desire for my faith to be large. In fact, I want it to be greater. But I want it to be a biblical one, where there is less of me and more of God.**

Word but by "speaking a word" to them, praying blessings over them, and proclaiming greater things over them and for them. It is "par for the American Christian course" to seek great things for ourselves and claim it is for God's glory. We often spiritualize our personal ambition, but the new prosperity takes it a step further and tries to use the victory of Jesus to declare it into existence. However, considering the lives of our faithful brothers and sisters in Scripture should correct this view. Yes, many of them experienced what we would identify as wonders or signs—"greater things." But these were always meant to point to something and Someone greater—in many cases, things that remained unseen in the believer's lifetime. The book of Hebrews speaks of our Old Testament family in this way:

> These all died in faith, although they had not received the things that were promised. But they saw them from a distance, greeted them, and confessed that they were foreigners and temporary residents on the earth. Now those who say such things make it clear that they are seeking a homeland. If they were thinking about where they came from, they would have had an opportunity to return. But they now desire a better place—a heavenly one. Therefore, God is not ashamed to be called their God, for he has prepared a city for them. (Heb. 11:13–16)

These saints didn't live on earth during the coming of the promised Messiah. They believed God's promises of redemption and looked ahead in the world to come. They were seeking a different world, a better one. They knew God had something greater prepared for them than what they could see here.

Pop-Christianity breeds a desire for God based on what

blessings He could give, more than delighting in God Himself. He is the means to a desired end. But if Christians are really looking out for our self-interest, the best thing we can possibly do is to pick up our crosses. As Matt Fuller succinctly puts it, "In life, and certainly in the Christian life, the mark of real maturity is to escape the prison of self-absorption."[8] There is a better goal worth living for than the temporary fulfillment of our fickle desires. And pleasure isn't even the enemy. God is not trying to rob us of satisfaction. Author Jon Bloom writes, "Pleasure is the meter in your heart that measures how valuable, how precious someone or something is to you. Pleasure is the measure of your treasure."[9] Thus we must ask ourselves if we delight in God's character or just His benefits.

Pastor Erik Raymond writes, "God is incessantly pursuing his own supremacy in all things, including the affections of us his creation."[10] God wants our affections based on who He is, before they are based on anything else. Dane Ortlund says that if we are going to be people who truly are about the gospel of Jesus Christ, we too must die. "We must die to our bookkeeping way of existence that builds our identity on anything other than Jesus. We must relinquish, give up on ourselves, throw in the towel."[11] I fear that pop-Christianity is setting up its followers for a faith crisis when everything doesn't go as dreamed.

Most readers here are probably familiar with the life of Job from the Old Testament. Job was a righteous man who endured extreme personal suffering. He cried out to God but remained firm in his assurance

> **Pop-Christianity breeds a desire for God based on what blessings He could give, more than delighting in God Himself.**

that whatever God was up to could be trusted. His posture of heart was, "The LORD gives, and the LORD takes away. Blessed be the name of the LORD" (Job 1:21). This is still true. Our God gives. And our God takes away. And if our churches do not prepare us for both, we are in discipleship danger zone. New prosperity gospel churches explain personal hardship as a sort of slingshot effect. God is preparing you for something greater or is going to "turn your setback into a comeback."

Some pastors do not even acquiesce that God is the one who allows hardship in the first place, as if He is having to play some sort of defensive strategy against bad things that happen to us. But the opening chapter of Job actually depicts God suggesting to Satan that he try and get Job to break, knowing that Job's faith would endure (Job 1:8). And God gives Satan parameters on what he can and cannot mess with in his endeavor (Job 1:12). That scenario is pretty upsetting to our modern sensibilities. But it is clear Scripture presents God as the one holding the reins. While the prosperity gospel of old would tell you to simply have more faith, the new prosperity gospel provides a pep talk of positivity, because "you're an overcomer."

But Job didn't assume that. He wasn't trying to leverage his hardship as equity with God. The account of his life records some of the worst things that could happen to someone. Yet we are told he grieved—"stood up, tore his robe, and shaved his head" (Job 1:20)—and still immediately "fell to the ground and worshiped" (v. 21). There was no God-sized dream to claim or vision from God to unlock. The only hope Job had in his anger, confusion, and tragedy was the object of his declaration of faith:

But I know that my Redeemer lives,
and at the end he will stand on the dust.

Even after my skin has been destroyed,
yet I will see God in my flesh.
I will see him myself;
my eyes will look at him, and not as a stranger.
My heart longs within me. (Job 19:25–27)

The longing of his heart was to see God. Singing "I know my Redeemer lives" in a worship set is a whole lot easier than believing it in worship when everything else has been taken away. We must understand that God does not owe us health, success, comfort, or privilege, and He does not promise them to us—at least not in the earthly ways we often long for. Martin Luther wrote of a "theology of glory" that "does not know God in suffering." It is an approach to Christianity and to life that tries

> in various ways to minimize difficult and painful things, or else to defeat and move past them, rather than looking them square in the face and accepting them. In particular, [this approach] acknowledge[s] the cross, but view[s] it primarily *as a means to an end*—an unpleasant but necessary step on the way to good things in the future . . . A sign that you are operating with a theology of glory is when your faith feels like a fight against these realities instead of a resource for accepting them.[12]

This is in contrast to a "theology of the cross" which "sees the cross as revealing the fundamental nature of God's involvement in the world this side of heaven."[13] I feel there is a discipleship crisis coming as the new prosperity gospel and its many iterations have insufficiently equipped people for a theology that includes hardship, death, failure, and a seeming lack of earthly "glory."

By all means, I believe there are people sitting in new prosperity churches who genuinely believe in the cross of Christ, and my hope for them is that the cross will increasingly be the place in which their absolute hope lies. A theology of the cross allows us in the worst circumstances to, as George Ladd wrote, cling to the truth that "death has been defeated; our conqueror has been conquered. In the face of the power of the Kingdom of God in Christ, death was helpless. . . . An empty tomb in Jerusalem is proof of it. This is the Gospel of the Kingdom."[14] This doesn't mean we want bad things to happen or should refrain from asking the Lord to take them away, but it means our faith grows to where we want to "know him and the power of his resurrection and the fellowship of his sufferings, being conformed to his death" (Phil. 3:10). My fear is that in the new prosperity, there is too often a resurrection without a cross.

> I feel there is a discipleship crisis coming as the new prosperity gospel and its many iterations have insufficiently equipped people for a theology that includes hardship, death, failure, and a seeming lack of earthly "glory."

Scott Hubbard says, "If you are in Christ, God will bear you up today. He will show you mercy. He will make you new. And when tomorrow comes, he will do it all again."[15] What great news we have to cling to as Christians! The victory we have in Jesus Christ is one that has spiked the ball not over trials but over death. In the meantime, as Jerry Bridges wrote, "God wants us to walk in *obedience*—not victory. Obedience is oriented toward God; victory is oriented toward self."[16] It is critical that we refuse to bypass God's sanctifying process of shaping us into the image of Christ. God is committed to the sanctification of His people. This means that our faith depends on what we can't see.

After the tragic death of his son, recording artist TobyMac posted a letter to the public stating:

> My wife and I would want the world to know this . . . We don't follow God because we have some sort of under-the-table deal with Him, like, we'll follow you if you bless us. We follow God because we love Him. It's our honor. He is the God of the hills and the valleys. And He is beautiful above all things.[17]

This is an "I know my Redeemer lives" faith. Let us rejoice and cling to the truth that the great blessing of God is God Himself. Let us join Paul in believing:

> Everything that was a gain to me, I have considered to be a loss because of Christ. More than that, I also consider every-thing to be a loss in view of the surpassing value of knowing Christ Jesus my Lord. Because of him I have suffered the loss of all things and consider them as dung, so that I may gain Christ and be found in him, not having a righteous-ness of my own from the law, but one that is through faith in Christ—the righteousness from God based on faith. My goal is to know him and the power of his resurrection and the fellowship of his sufferings, being conformed to his death, assuming that I will somehow reach the resurrection from among the dead. (Phil. 3:7–11)

10

Curb Your Enthusiasm:

The Unmet Expectations of the New Prosperity Gospel

Be content to suffer, to die, and to be forgotten.
—NIKOLAUS ZINZENDORF

Ron Powlus was the top-ranked quarterback in all of high school football. Every college in America wanted the Pennsylvania senior to be their future quarterback. Powlus signed with Notre Dame and arrived on campus in South Bend, Indiana, in the early 1990s. He made his first start against Northwestern as a freshman, which was a very rare occurrence at the time for an elite school. Powlus performed as advertised, throwing for several touchdowns in the Irish victory.

Later that evening on ESPN's SportsCenter, famed college football columnist Beano Cook was interviewed about the new Notre Dame quarterback. What Cook predicted would be a stigma against Ron Powlus throughout his career: Cook claimed that not only would Ron Powlus win the Heisman Trophy, but he would win it twice. (Only Ohio State's Archie Griffin had won two Heisman trophies before and that is still the case.) Cook made this prediction after one game! Powlus never won a Heisman trophy and actually didn't even come close.

His career was considered a disappointment, a "bust," by most fans who remember him. What's ridiculous about that view of Powlus's Notre Dame career is that he still graduated as the all-time leading passer in Notre Dame history and held on to the record for more than a decade after his career was over. When you combine his high-profile ranking coming out of high school with Beano Cook's prediction, Powlus seemed worse than he actually was and is remembered as such. He was simply the product of unrealistic expectations.

A college freshman isn't even comparable to the almighty God, but I believe that disappointment with God is inevitable for those who have formed their own expectations of how God should be—those who live their Christian lives holding Him to promises He didn't make or misleading ideas they've been taught about what a truly loving God would do for them. As my favorite sports radio host Colin Cowherd says, "Happiness is controlled by expectations."

Christians in America too often expect that by doing all the right things, God will bless us with the American Dream.[1] But the Christian life is never presented in the Scriptures as a life of ease. It is a life of struggle, a "long obedience in the same direction," as Eugene Peterson popularized. There's a reason the book of Hebrews instructs us to "run with endurance the race that lies before us" (Heb. 12:1). However cliché to say, the process of working out our salvation really is a marathon and not a sprint. When life doesn't work out exactly as we planned or hoped, an important question to ask ourselves is, "What did you expect?"

Jackie Knapp has written that many have had expectations for their twenties that were not rooted in reality. This can be true in terms of relationships, finances, houses, travel, career, and love. When disappointment or emptiness or tragedy strike, it is easy to blame God when we were imagining it was our allegiance to Him that would shield us from hardship. Knapp admits, "We need to take responsibility for our role in our delusions, buying into pop Christian culture instead of the Bible, believing the larger cultural claims that youth is the highest good."[2] The call of God in the Scriptures is not for those with shattered dreams or unmet expectations to just suck it up or get over it but rather to turn to the actual promises of God as their hope, realigning expectations to what He has already told us in His Word. Don't get me wrong; we should have expectations that God keeps His word. This is the ultimate Christian expectation, grounded in our certain hope in Christ. The issue is when we either don't know what His Word says or hold Him hostage to promises that either were not for us or that He never made.

It is important to know that Eeyore from *Winnie-the-Pooh* is not the Christian posture we're trying to model. We don't expect gloom; rather, we expect to live in a world that is broken, and not our ultimate home. We need to put to death our expectations of a perfect earthly life, prepare for things to be hard, and realize the fall has affected every part of the world.

When I stay overnight at someone else's home while traveling, it may be a nice experience, but the sleep is never the same as being in my own bed. I know my sleep won't be as good as being in my own house, and while that's not ideal, I know I'll be home soon, so it's okay. Someone else's home should never feel like it is our own. We are guests, there temporarily. As Christians, we must realize that this earth is not our home. There is a world to come,

> **The call of God in the Scriptures is not for those with shattered dreams or unmet expectations to just suck it up or get over it but rather to turn to the actual promises of God as their hope.**

where everything will eventually make sense, be repaired, and feel right. In fact, it will be perfect. It will exceed our expectations and deepest longings. The apostle Paul, the same man who wrote about contentment in Christ, also claimed, "For I consider that the sufferings of this present time are not worth comparing with the glory that is going to be revealed to us" (Rom. 8:18).

Paul had massive expectations for the glory that was going to come, and it allowed the sufferings and struggles of this life to take their proper place in the relative scheme of things. He expected what God promised him to come true, and so should all Christians.

Missionary William Carey famously said, "Expect great things from God. Attempt great things for God." Is Carey giving unbiblical advice? The apostle Paul wrote: "Now to him who is able to do above and beyond all that we ask or think according to the power that works in us—to him be glory in the church and in Christ Jesus to all generations, forever and ever. Amen" (Eph. 3:20–21). Commenting on this, Matt Perman notes that focusing on who wrote Ephesians 3 is critical to evaluating and understanding Carey's charge to believers. "Paul accomplished far-reaching and incredible things for the gospel—to the point where he was even able to say that 'from Jerusalem and all the way around to Illyricum I have fulfilled the ministry of the gospel of Christ' (Romans 15:19). In other words, he attempted great things for God (and accomplished them!)."[3] The key is that Paul was acting and praying and believing in line with God's preexisting assignment to send Paul to the nations with the gospel. Perman continues, "So, attempt great things for God—grounding all of your efforts and labor and dreams in God's grace, supported by prayer, just like Ephesians 3:20 says."[4]

How different is this than going after what you declare to be great things and expecting God to endorse them and give His blessing. Paul's great dream jumps off the pages of all his letters. He wanted to know Jesus more and for others to have the same opportunity. He wanted healthy churches and sound doctrine. Further, I'd be remiss if I didn't emphasize that Paul was carrying out a direct assignment from Jesus (outlined in Acts and Ephesians, among other places). He was aiming to carry out God's will. Could that have been a tremendous contributor to the "greatness" of his ministry efforts? We are not apostles, but God's Word shows us what mission our God is on and what efforts He intends to support. We, too, must be walking in line with the commands of Scripture—that's where we can find our direction! His Word is a lamp unto our feet (Ps. 119:105), shedding light on the proper paths.

William Carey (who said we should expect great things from God) was a missionary. The great thing he expected from God and attempted for God was for God's gospel to go out to the nations. In response to the lack of missional urgency he perceived from fellow believers, Carey wrote a work he called *An Enquiry into the Obligations of Christians to Use Means for the Conversion of the Heathens*. What a title. In it, he bemoaned, "Multitudes sit at ease, and give themselves no concern about the far greater part of their fellow-sinners, who to this day, are lost in ignorance and idolatry."[5] It was at the inaugural meeting of a missionary society that he organized where Carey spoke the words memorialized centuries later: "Expect great things from God; attempt great things for God!"[6] The great things he expected and attempted were outworkings of the Great Commission—indeed, the greater things that Jesus promised His disciples. Guy Richard writes:

> The fact that Christians were not attempting great things for God indicated that they were not expecting Him to do great things in and through them. They may well have known that God was "able to do far more abundantly than all" they asked or even thought (Eph. 3:20), but they were obviously not expecting that He would actually do so in point of fact. Their actions, or, more accurately, their lack of actions, showed that they believed they were living in a day of small things. And that is why Carey's sermon challenged them to think bigger and to expect more from God. He knew that if and when they did, they would begin to step out in faith and take risks for the cause of Christ.[7]

I must ask myself what "great things" I have attempted for God and if those things are truly focused on the Great Commission or on my own ambition. If I could ask God one thing and one thing only, I hope my ask would be for the soul of one who doesn't know the Lord. I want to pray with expectation that God is going to move in my city and save souls. I can't be diligent and persistent in that prayer if I am consumed with my expectations for what God should be doing in my life.

There are many promises of

> **I must ask myself what "great things" I have attempted for God and if those things are truly focused on the Great Commission or on my own ambition.**

God that we can expect Him to fulfill. About these promises, Erik Raymond says, "Every moment of every day is an opportunity to declare our abiding faith in God and his promises. Each day is filled with any number of tough choices that we have to make that demonstrate if we are believing God or not."[8] He then asks, "Are you all in on God's promises?" I hope I am, and want to give you a list of some of my favorite promises from God, applicable to every believer in Christ:

> He will never cast me out. (John 6:37)
> He will be faithful to carry out the work He started in me.
> (Phil. 1:6)
> He will be with me until the end of the age. (Matt. 28:20)
> The gates of hell will not prevail against His church.
> (Matt. 16:18)
> His Word can equip me for every good work.
> (2 Tim. 3:16–17)
> He gives me peace that surpasses all understanding.
> (Phil. 4:7)
> He cares more about me than about the birds of the air, for
> which He provides in abundance. (Matt. 6:26)
> He will forgive my sins and remove them from me as far as
> the east is from the west. (Ps. 103:12)
> He has made me a new creation. (2 Cor. 5:17)
> I have been justified by faith. (Rom. 5:1–2)
> He will not waste the suffering and trials in my life.
> (James 1:3–4)
> He has adopted me into His family. (Eph. 1:5)
> Jesus will come again. (1 Cor. 15:23)
> He will give me eternal life. (John 3:16)

What I love about these promises is that any Christian, any-where, in any time in history, can equally claim and expect these to be true. A Christian facing the death penalty for owning a Bible in a country hostile toward the gospel, where it is illegal to be a Chris-tian, can claim those promises and have an expectation for them all to be true to the same extent as someone leading worship in front of thousands of people at a conference in downtown Nashville, Tennessee. All who are in Christ rest in the promise that "those he predestined, he also called; and those he called, he also justified; and those he justified, he also glorified" (Rom. 8:30).

"What, then, are we to say about these things?" writes the apostle Paul. "If God is for us, who is against us?" (Rom. 8:31). God never promises us a spouse, downtown high-rise apartment, a platform, influence, children, or a church that checks every box. He did promise us that nothing can separate us from the love of Christ (Rom. 8:38–39). Instead of holding God hostage to promises He never made, let us worship Him with brothers and sisters of all languages, back-grounds, financial statuses, and experiences for the promises He has made to us in Christ, in whom every promise is Yes.

> **Instead of holding God hostage to promises He never made, let us worship Him with brothers and sisters of all languages, backgrounds, financial statuses, and experiences for the promises He has made to us in Christ, in whom every promise is Yes.**

I was once asked to be the commencement speaker for a Christian high school graduation. It was a privilege to encourage the graduates before they set off to the rest of their lives, and I was honored to be there. But my message was not the "you can change the world" charge the room was expecting. I stepped to the microphone and told the graduates, "Most of you have been told this week that you have unlimited potential. I'm here to tell you that you're being lied to. In fact, reality shows the opposite. You have incredibly limited potential. The good news is that you serve a God with zero limits, and He has a mission He wants you to be part of that actually does have unlimited potential. 'So expect great things from God, and attempt great things for God,' to the ends of the earth." Turn your tassels to that, and let's go.

11

The Great Escape:
Aftermath of Pop-Christian Discipleship

The whole of the believer's life
is lived under the shadow of the cross
and in the warm glow of the empty grave.
—ALEX KOCMAN

My friend pastors a church within a par-5 golf shot of a large and well-known new prosperity church. His church is serious about preaching the gospel, and the redemptive work of Christ is what shapes their entire idea of discipleship. In recent years, my friend has noticed a trend of people showing up to his church from the prosperity church next door, admitting they've been starved for sound discipleship and biblical preaching. Internally, my friend's staff has begun referring to these people as "refugees," recognizing the urgency to help them recover from hearing a misleading gospel focused on an American spin on the blessings of God.

These people are craving something different and lasting, and it has nothing to do with style of church music or personal preference. Ray Ortlund notes that there is a need "more pro-found than a momentary upsurge of enthusiasm."[1] The need is nothing less than the re-Christianization of their discipleship, ac-cording to the gospel alone, by Christ Himself.

Jesus and His redemptive work must become the focus of not just their salvation but also their sanctification. Anything else will certainly leave a Christian malnourished, headed for a place where a diet of nothing but sugar and sweets will take its toll. New prosper-ity churches are doctrinal candy stores. Amy Gannett writes about the lack of scriptural nutrition she experienced in pop-Christianity, reflecting that "Christians frequently exchange the nourishing truths of God's Word for 'sweeter' substitutes." Gannett writes:

> I've leaned on Pinterest-worthy quotes about how I'm an
> overcomer who can do anything. In times of spiritual drought,
> I've listened to social-media influencers tell me I already
> have everything I need within myself. And in times of chaos,
> I've cherished well-intended words from friends reminding
> me that I'm already stronger than I could ever believe.[2]

But, Gannett says:

> These tasty mantras aren't telling me the whole truth. . . .
> They tell me I'm strong, but do nothing to remind me of
> God's true strength (Isa. 41:10). They tell me I'm capable,
> but neglect to tell me God is the source of all things (James
> 1:17). They tell me I'm enough, but fail to remind me that he
> is the eternal "I AM" (Ex. 3:14). They tell me I can do more
> than I really can. They lure me into thinking they offer lasting
> nourishment, only to leave me exhausted, defeated, and
> looking for my next fix.[3]

John Owen is known to have said, "Christ is the meat, the bread, the food of our souls. Nothing is in Him of a higher spiritual nourishment than His love, which we should always desire."[4] Anything else is like drinking homemade lemonade when you're really thirsty on a hot day. That drink tastes fantastic, but what happens a few minutes after? You're thirsty. Jesus said, "Whoever drinks from the water that I will give him will never get thirsty again" (John 4:14).

Despite the engaging services and "authentic" discipleship experiences found in many popular churches, there is a sort of aftermath that leaves people wondering what could be missing. The solution is not less authenticity, or even less enthusiasm, but gospel-centrality. While gospel-centrality can be a buzzword in certain circles, I appreciate Joe Thorn's definition: "The gospel-centered *life* is a life where a Christian experiences a growing personal reliance on the gospel that protects him from depending on his own religious performance and being seduced and overwhelmed by idols."[5] A gospel-centered life leads our focus away from our own efforts of self-righteousness and away from the worship of things other than God. Thorn writes:

> The gospel—and Jesus himself—is our greatest hope and boast, our deepest longing and joy, and our most passionate song and message. It means that the gospel is what defines us as Christians, unites us as brothers and sisters, changes us as sinner/saints and sends us as God's people on mission. When we are gospel-centered the gospel is exalted above every other good thing in our lives and triumphs over every bad thing set against it.[6]

Gospel-centrality must not be, as Alex Kocman aptly noted, reduced to a moment of powerful emotional experience: "Those who grew up within the traditions of revivalism and soul-winning know how quickly the multi-faceted, face-melting glory of the gospel can be flattened into a dull, regurgitated sales pitch."[7] We must, as church leaders and members, remember that we are in this together as a single body Christ is building. Our personal behaviors and sanctification have communal impacts. It is the church that carries out God's mission, and that is not possible with only an army of confused consumers.

The book of Ephesians gives us a profound look into the overall mission and intentions of God throughout history, uncovering a staggering truth about the church itself. In Ephesians 2, Paul outlines that despite Israel's belief in a coming Jewish political power, God was instead making a "new man" (the unified church) made of Jews and Gentiles, anyone who would believe in Christ for salvation—from every tribe, tongue, and nation. It is this single body (the church) of whom Christ is the "cornerstone" (v. 20), "being put together" (v. 21), "being built together for God's dwelling" (v. 22). And here comes another staggering revelation. Ephesians 3:10–12 tells us that this creation of the glorious church is "so that God's multi-faceted wisdom may now *be made known through the church to the rulers and authorities in the heavens.* This is according to his eternal purpose accomplished in Christ Jesus our Lord. In him we have boldness and confident access through faith in him." Paul is declaring that our witness as a global church is the means by which the world around us and the angels and demons in the spiritual realm are seeing the unfolding glory of God's plan to redeem creation.

It makes sense of Ephesians 4–6, in which Paul addresses Christian ethics, marriage, social propriety, and culminates with the armor of God. This is our mission! This is why we need God's power; this is why we can ask Him for "great things," and this is why discipleship matters. We feel destined for amazing things? What could be a more incredible and worthy cause? We are in this together, and we are the gatekeepers of "mysteries" once hidden and now given to the church. This glorious truth should be like a jetpack that fuels our local and global church efforts. John Stott writes:

> **It is the church that carries out God's mission, and that is not possible with only an army of confused consumers.**

> The good news of the unsearchable riches of Christ which Paul preached is that he died and rose again not only to save sinners like me (though he did), but also to create a single new humanity; not only to redeem us from sin but also to adopt us into God's family; not only to reconcile us to God but also to reconcile us to one another. Thus the church is an integral part of the gospel. The gospel is good news of a new society as well as of a new life.

> If . . . (like Paul) we keep before us the vision of God's new society as his family, his dwelling place and his instrument in the world, then we shall constantly be seeking to make our church's worship more authentic, its fellowship more caring and its outreach more compassionate. In other words (like Paul again), we shall be ready to pray, to work and if necessary to suffer in order to turn the vision into a reality.[8]

With this incredible vision in mind, let us avoid falling into some common ditches that can consume our local church efforts.

Emphasis on Numbers

While I appreciate efforts and a passion to get as many people to church as possible, and I share that passion, if numbers alone drive a church, pragmatism will win the day. Early on in pastoring the church I planted with a group of friends, I had a "whatever it takes" mentality to get someone to church. While I still feel that way, what has changed is what I believe *it actually takes* to get people to come to church. Many new prosperity methods (some of which I've tried) are perfectly designed to attract either people who don't think their current church is cool or exciting enough or cultural Christians who want a church that isn't going to talk about much that will make them uncomfortable.

These churches don't usually attract classic "unchurched" unbelievers, even if they are aiming to do so. Why would someone who isn't a Christian decide to show up because your band does a popular secular song to open the service? Do we really think an unbeliever cares about that? I've learned from experience that most actually think that is strange. Has an unbeliever ever cared how a pastor dressed? Are they really going to show up to church after years or even a lifetime of being unchurched because they heard about the pastor's admirable collection of expensive sneakers? I've still never met that unchurched person who cares.

You know who cares? People who are already part of the church. In the celebrity pastor culture of pop-Christianity, the coolness of the pastor and the church is an important matter to the gathering of fans. But, be warned, "The truth of a teacher's words is determined not by the feats he can perform but by the orthodoxy of what he teaches. We are never to follow anyone who perverts the truth of God's Word, no matter how gifted that person is, how large of an organization that person commands, or how amazing that person's work seems to be."[9]

The numbers-driven church can also be described as an "entertainment-driven" church. Owen Strachan writes, "We say we are following the God of heaven, but when you look at [many church] services, you might see knock-off versions of worldly impressiveness, uniqueness, thinking, and entertainment."[10] When it comes to getting unchurched unbelievers to come to church, it isn't the cool factor or the latest marketing strategy that proves effective. It is the arm of a trusted friend who is living their life on mission and has invested genuine care into the friendship. Imagine telling an atheist friend, "Our pastor dresses so awesome. He doesn't look like other pastors." Or, "Our church is giving away a free iPad at Easter. You should come." Someone truly on mission is not in the marketing business but is about relationships, not clever tactics. In his modern-day classic, *The Courage to Be Protestant*, David Wells writes:

[The] marketing church has calculated that unless it makes deep, serious cultural adaptations, it will go out of business, especially with the younger generations. What it has not considered carefully enough is that it may well be putting itself out of business with God. And the further irony is that the younger generations who are less impressed by whiz-bang technology, who often see through what is slick and glitzy, and who have been on the receiving end of enough marketing to nauseate them, are as likely to walk away from these oh-so-relevant churches as to walk into them.[11]

Emphasis on Self-Help

Numbers-driven and self-help-driven churches can be considered twins. One has a little more glitz, the other a little more guru. The self-help focus finds its ancestry in the seeker-sensitive church movement of the 1980s and '90s, where "felt needs" drove content strategy for Sunday sermons and small group discussion guides. Kyle Strobel notes that one must begin with the word "self," in self-help, to see immediately how problematic this approach to ministry is for the church. He says, "The second we give ourselves to self-help, we are capitulating to a culture that assumes that self is centered, and now I just give myself to things to better myself, to identify myself."[12] The way of Christian discipleship is not one of self-discovery but Christ-discovery. Strobel continues, "If you want to discover yourself, you discover yourself in Christ."[13]

Should preaching allow the hearer room for personal application points and personal takeaways? Absolutely, but we must be first equipping people with truth as God presents it in the Scriptures. One of my seminary professors advised us to "never preach a sermon that would still be true if Jesus had not died and risen again." When self-improvement is the focus, going to church feels like being assigned a New Year's resolution every week. When it is simply about improving life or attempting to become more moral, it is easy to forget, as Trevin Wax says, "the fundamental truths":

The way of Christian discipleship is not one of self-discovery but Christ-discovery.

The goodness of creation, the holiness of God, the reality of sin, the suddenness of suffering, the inevitability of death, and the need for salvation. We create the illusion that we are in control, and we expect the church to come alongside us with tips for better living, something that will sweeten the life we've cooked up for ourselves.[14]

Actually caring for the self in appropriate ways is not the enemy—I'm not advocating for a harsh or obtuse approach to emotional or mental care. But as Christians (especially pastors), we must never provide self-help principles as a gospel substitute. We know that they are not one. Amie Patrick candidly notes, "While I've deeply resonated with much of the common sense in the philosophy of self-care, other aspects have troubled me and seem completely incompatible with Christianity. I couldn't agree with Scripture and at the same time agree with arguments encouraging me to pursue a self-focused, indulgent, comfort-based lifestyle."[15]

Eventually, a follower of Christ has to come to a crossroads and either acknowledge that much of what we are seeing in our culture regarding the priority of the self is contradictory to Scripture (and choose one to live by!) or justify it by merging it into the faith, which has become the common practice in pop-Christianity. God forbid that the church becomes the place where this hybrid product is peddled.

Wax describes the great temptation for churches today to try to draw crowds by serving up sweets over sustenance. Just give people what they like the most, whether it's the catchiest song, self-help book or Bible study, or a sermon series that chases the latest fad. The truth is that what people like and even crave in the moment is often not what they actually need. Sadly, self-help church (under the banner of being seeker-friendly or sensitive) almost always means softening difficult doctrines or ignoring them altogether. The felt need isn't the actual need.

Emphasis on Authenticity

This one is hard to define, but it is definitely "a thing." The greatest value of our day seems to be authenticity. In Christian circles, this usually means people are readily willing to admit how broken and imperfect they are. (Pastor, if you want to get the applause of many, make sure you tell the church how much you don't have it together.) But authenticity itself is not a firm foundation: "A number of studies have shown that people's *feelings* of authenticity are often shaped by something other than their loyalty to their unique qualities. Paradoxically, feelings of authenticity seem to be related to a kind of social conformity."[16] When it is the social convention to be authentic, we get in line to make sure we are viewed that way, especially if it is tied to spirituality. But let's be real: we can be "authentic" about our sin and still not repent of it. But true repentance is necessary for the believer. An authenticity-driven church wants you to repent of not being your true self. Not that we have any idea what that actually means. Author Emma Scrivener isn't a huge fan of the modern-day concept of authenticity, especially in the church. She posted the following memes she's come across about being authentic:

> "By choosing to be our most authentic self, we leave a trail of magic wherever we go."
> "There is nothing more beautiful than your authentic self."
> "People who are true to their authentic selves have found the secret to ultimate happiness."[17]

Honestly, those make me ill. I'm glad I didn't eat before I wrote this section. Scrivener asks to which self we're supposed to be true: "The self who doesn't do repentance; or discomfort or a crucified God?" She answers, "Sure—I can be true to this self. But I can tell you, it won't leave a trail of magic."[18] It seems that no matter how much the world celebrates authenticity, it doesn't know how to find the real thing.

Often the more authentic someone appears, the less authentic they are, (the Instagrammer who spends forever on her "no makeup" selfie; the guy who bares his soul as a [pick-up] technique; the marketer who sells shabby chic as a brand)....

While the culture may tell me to seek the world's validation for my authentic self, the gospel tells me to seek Jesus' forgiveness for my inexcusable sins. There's a big difference.[19]

In an authenticity-driven church, "brokenness" is preferred over "sin." As a result, the magnitude of our status as sinners is underplayed, and the restorative state of our redemption is not fully realized. The reality is, as a Christian you aren't a broken mess anymore—you have been washed, renewed, and made righteous. I wish there would be as much conversation about how redeemed we are by Christ as there is how broken we are. When we do sin, we need more gospel that leads to repentance, not more socially conventional authenticity that leads to group therapy.

Christ crucified and risen is what should drive the preaching, discipleship, and everything else about our faith and local churches. Pastor and friend Tony Merida says that anything less is "Christianity-lite." He writes, "Leadership talks, therapeutic sermons, and practical-improvement messages fill the air."[20] They make fans, not disciples. Tony describes the proper goal, a gospel-centered church, with some examples:

> **The reality is, as a Christian you aren't a broken mess anymore—you have been washed, renewed, and made righteous.**

[Gospel-centered] churches preach the gospel every week explicitly—but not just to the unbeliever. They also preach and apply the gospel to Christians, as Paul did for the Romans (Rom. 1:15). It shapes and empowers Christian ethics and the life of the Christian community.

For example, marriage is taught by looking at Christ's love for the church (Eph. 5:25); generosity is viewed through the lens of Christ's generosity (2 Cor. 8:9); the call to forgive is rooted in Christ's forgiveness of us (Col. 3:13); hospitality reflects the welcome of Christ (Rom. 15:7). Calls to social action—like caring for the orphan, the widow, the refugee, and the poor—are also made to believers with reference to their own identity in Christ.[21]

Merida quotes Charles Spurgeon: "Keep to the gospel, then, more and more. Give the people Christ and nothing but Christ. Satiate them, even though some should say that you also nauseate them, with the gospel. . . . By the roadside, in the little room, in the theater—anywhere, everywhere, let us preach Christ."[22]

So let's be honest here as Christians, and especially anyone reading with pastoral or administrative influence in the leadership of a church: If the gospel—if "satiating" people with Christ and Christ alone—is not the center of all of our efforts, where is our confidence placed? The only honest (or, if you prefer, authentic) answer is ourselves. Dr. Martyn Lloyd-Jones taught that there's a big difference between advice and news, emphasizing that the gospel is good news, not good advice.

Tim Keller summarizes Lloyd-Jones's distinction this way: "Advice is counsel about something to do, and it hasn't happened yet, but you can do it. . . . News is a report about something that has happened yet. You can't do anything about. It's been done for you, and all you can do is respond to it."[23] Like the church "refugees" my friend's congregation is receiving, let's hope that anyone who has been misled by a false gospel will realize they actually don't have what it takes. Or that they will tire of moralism, or the inspirational, or the therapeutic. And let's pray that we are waiting there with refreshing gospel nourishment and Christ-centered community to welcome

> When we do sin, we need more gospel that leads to repentance, not more socially conventional authenticity that leads to group therapy.

them. We've got news to share. And as Martyn Lloyd-Jones would say, "The business of preaching is to make such knowledge live."[24]

12

Most Likely to Succeed:
Pursuing Godly Ambition

You don't have to be the greatest . . . anything . . . that ever lived.
Rest and trust in a God who delights in and blesses
an ordinary life lived well.
—BART BARBER

Is personal ambition bad for the Christian?

It depends. In certain arenas, one should only start if success is the goal. When someone studies for their entrance exam into law or medical school, I would guess that they have some sort of ambition to become an attorney or a doctor and that they most likely desire a successful practice. The entrepreneur doesn't launch a business hoping to just break even financially. And as a former church planter, I have never met anyone who sets out to start a church hoping the impact will be minimal. When my friends and I decided to start our church, we had high hopes of reaching a lot of people for Christ and sending church members across the globe to make a worldwide impact. We weren't aiming for a few friends having a house church.

Pastor Dan Dodds wrote that in Scripture, "The word *ambition* is employed in both positive and negative contexts. Negatively, James condemns those who have 'bitter jealousy and selfish ambition' (James 3:14). Positively, Paul 'makes it [his] ambition to preach the gospel' (Rom. 15:20). Clearly, the Bible acknowledges both good and bad ambition. How do we know the difference?"[1]

My friend Matt Smethurst wrote, "One thing that separates biblical Christianity from almost every other religion is its laser-like focus on our hearts. Our Creator cares what we do, to be sure, but most fundamentally he cares how and *why* we do certain things. He's interested in those intentions that are hidden from human eyes."[2] Motives matter. (Ironically, Matt's article is about why our message matters *more* than our motives—we can be sincere and be sincerely wrong—but I think we've belabored that point in this book.)

When I watch a crime drama, one of the keys to solving the crime is establishing a motive. This can narrow down the search for suspects. When it comes to personal ambition, even in good goals such as growing a ministry or running a thriving business, motive matters to God. As we examine our own hearts, we must launch an investigation to identify our motives.

Further, our ambitions need proper direction and grounding. Pastor Dave Harvey wrote a helpful booked called *Rescuing Ambition*. I think there are immediate takeaways from the title alone. He didn't say to avoid ambition or to run full speed ahead in hustle. He said ambition needs to be rescued. There is a good kind and a bad kind, and rather than urge ambitious Christians to suppress all their drive, Dave suggests instead that it needs guardrails.

If you've ever driven on mountain roads, you know that guardrails not only protect drivers and passengers, they also make it easier to keep a good speed. My family goes to the North Carolina mountains every summer, and we love to drive on the Blue Ridge Parkway. The winding sections of that drive without guardrails cause me to slow down, take exceeding caution, and (honestly) freak out. But when there are guardrails, I can more comfortably keep a good pace and stay in the lane. Similarly, we can press the gas on ambition a bit more confidently when the proper guardrails are lining the roads, helping us avoid an unhindered, unsafe, and undirected trajectory.

So what are these guardrails? The apostle Paul commands: "Do nothing out of selfish ambition or conceit, but in humility consider others as more important than yourselves. Everyone should look not to his own interests, but rather to the interests of others" (Phil. 2:3–4). Do *nothing* out of selfish ambition. But instead look to the interests of others. So we know our efforts are to be done in humility and for a purpose. We know we are to work to glorify God and serve others.

Without the guardrails of humility, ambition can quickly redirect Christians from living as servants of God to living as servants of their own desires. This will be a battle for as long as we are on this earth, because "selfish ambition is a sin that always seems to be 'crouching at the door' (Genesis 4:7)."[3] In *Rescuing Ambitions*, Dave Harvey says guardrails keep us on God's road and move in the direction of His glory. This is the very thing we should be seeking— God's glory. If you're into sports, politics, wrestling, or even Star Wars, you know what a rivalry is. Consider this: In our own lives, God's glory versus our own is the ultimate rivalry. It makes pairings like Alabama vs. Auburn, the Red Sox vs. the Yankees, and Republicans vs. Democrats look like they are holding hands and skipping in a field. We cannot be simultaneously glorifying God and glorifying ourselves. We cannot even aim to blend them just a little bit.

Godly ambition requires the discipline of turning our eyes to Christ and evaluating our own motives. God wants us to think sensibly (Rom. 12:3). This begins by not being conformed to the patterns of the world (Rom. 12:2), being transformed by the renewing of our minds (Rom. 12:2), and not thinking of ourselves more highly than we should (Rom. 12:3). Paul modeled this recovery of ambition, resolving, "We make it our aim to be pleasing to him" (2 Cor. 5:9). This was the ambition that consumed Paul. Since Jesus had taken hold of him (Phil. 3:12), Paul's ambition was to pursue Christ even more.

Without the guardrails of humility, ambition can quickly redirect Christians from living as servants of God to living as servants of their own desires.

I once was asked to be the guest speaker for a visiting team at a college football chapel service. The team had a 0-10 record on the season and was about to play a top ten team in the nation. In other words, it was gonna get ugly. They weren't just going to lose; someone was going to get hurt. In that situation, the typical player's ambition is making it back home for Christmas break in one piece. I wasn't sure how many on the team were Christians, but I decided to speak directly to those who knew the Lord. I told them, "You have a reason to play tomorrow. You have motivation to hustle on the field. And you have all you need for purpose going into the game: you are playing for the glory of God." Win or lose, we as Christians have different goals than the world around us. Our goals are aimed at worshiping God and using our opportunities for His glory. You know what? Sometimes that means losing well.

By the time Chuck Colson, aide to disgraced President Richard

Nixon of the Watergate scandal, was released from prison, Colson was a follower of Jesus Christ. The disgrace was gone, and he was a new creation. He founded Prison Fellowship, a ministry that has advocated for prison reform and has led thousands to faith in Christ while serving their sentences in prison. Describing the difference between his life before Christ and his new life as a repentant believer, Colson reflected, "I was ambitious, and I am ambitious today, but I hope it is not for Chuck Colson (though I struggle quite a lot as a matter of fact). But I am ambitious for Christ."[4] The reality is that there is no nuance or "both/and" for the person committed to following Jesus. Either we will be ambitious for ourselves or ambitious for Christ. He must increase; I must decrease.

In an article entitled "The Disease of Ambition," Bruce Baugus wrote, "Selfish ambition, at least to a certain degree, is not only an acceptable sin in our culture but a seemingly necessary one for success. It may also be incentivized in a church culture caving to the temptation of elevating a public image of success."[5] By contrast, "Godly ambition does not promote any cult of personality, but selflessly serves Christ and his Church, and seeks no other prize than his glory and what he has promised in the Gospel. Paul's ambition, therefore, drives him to acts of profound and costly self-denial in order to fulfill his mission."[6]

Advocating for ambition for Christ over ourselves does not mean we sit at home and never pursue natural giftings or interests. It's certainly not "not trying." This couldn't be further from the truth. It's just a call not to fall into idolatry. Consider money, as an example. The Scriptures don't say that money is evil. Money is what God uses to fund His mission around the world. It is used to help many who are suffering, build churches for saints to gather in worship, plant churches, and send kids to life-changing youth camps. There is a long list of good and important things made possible by financial generosity. Money is not, as commonly misattributed, the "root of all evil." It is the *love* of money that is the root of all evil (1 Tim. 6:10). John Piper has explained this verse by saying that money "is of no value in itself (the paper or the metal). It is desirable only because it is a cultural symbol which can be traded for the 'many desires' that we have. But it cannot be traded for God or godliness. Therefore, the love of money in Paul's mind corresponds to the root longing for the things money can buy minus God. That is why all these *many desires* 'plunge people into ruin and destruction' (verse 9)."[7] In short, money can buy anything but God, so to be enslaved to it is to miss God altogether.

James draws a similar distinction about ambition. "For where there is envy and selfish ambition, there is disorder and every evil practice" (James 3:16). Every evil practice. It seems these idols of success and glory are gateway drugs to all manner of chaos. Misplaced ambition can cause otherwise-faithful Christians to find themselves seeking a bigger platform, abandoning gospel-centrality for more influential or popular teaching, or chasing experiences that will scratch every itch of desired success.

Misplaced ambition also breeds great insecurity. I see it in the church, with people wondering why they don't get to sing as many songs as someone else, or why they weren't on the schedule to be on stage at Easter, or why the pastor doesn't notice them as much as someone else. I see it in the desire to make one's church more like one they follow on Instagram, wanting their church to be as cool as what they get to see on their phones from another city. When the focus is on ourselves, traps of comparison inevitably follow. Others can become competition, standing in the way of your insecurity masked as pursuit of full potential.

Author Kristen Wetherell answers the question of whether

Christians can be ambitious in a way that pleases God. She exclaims, "Yes! Christ lived, died, and resurrected to free us from bondage to selfish ambition and vanity, giving us a purpose beyond merely making ourselves comfortable, happy, rich, and well-liked."[8] Isn't that great news?

I believe there are questions we can ask ourselves regarding personal ambition to serve as guardrails. Inspired by a C. S. Lewis address to King's College graduates, my friend Eric Geiger lays out three important ones: 1) Whose name will be made great? 2) Why am I so driven? and 3) How is my ambition expressed?[9]

> **Misplaced ambition can cause otherwise-faithful Christians to find themselves seeking a bigger platform, abandoning gospel-centrality for more influential or popular teaching, or chasing experiences that will scratch every itch of desired success.**

Whose Name Will Be Made Great?

We have to ask this question. I don't even think it can be answered quickly. Whose name is being elevated? As a pastor of a large church, who wrote the book you are holding in your hands, I often get my name elevated. There is a temptation to want even more of it. Who doesn't like hearing their name? I regularly have to fight the pull to make my name great. The best remedy is to ask myself, "Great in the eyes of whom?" God isn't impressed by any accolades, book sales, or speaking engagements. Neither is my wife. If only I could insert a shoulder shrug emoji here. In writing this very book I had to ask myself why I am doing it. What is my ambition? My hope is that my motives are pure and that it will be a tool for the church in understanding how a less-than-full gospel has infiltrated Christianity and how true devotion to Christ is the only solution. I hope my motivation is to elevate Christ over the wisdom of the world. It is easy for that to change by the day, so I must walk carefully, staying within the guardrails.

There are other ambitions that I believe to be pure, some of which are wanting to earn a certain income to provide for your family, retire without being a burden to your children, leave your future grandchildren an inheritance, etc. Those are wonderful ambitions. But how do they stay in check? By grace we must remember to ask ourselves, "Who makes you so superior? What do you have that you didn't receive?" (1 Cor. 4:7). God is the giver. We are not entitled to our abilities, and our accomplishments are not the reward. God's glory is our reward. Anything less is selfish ambition.

Why Am I So Driven?

So what exactly is motivating me? I wish we would ask that question more of the church member who spends several minutes editing a selfie before it is posted. What's driving that? It's not new. When the Galatians were giving in to the false gospel of circumcision being required for Gentile believers to receive salvation, Paul asked them, "For am I now trying to persuade people, or God? Or am I striving to please people? If I were still trying to please people, I would not be a servant of Christ" (Gal. 1:10). Circumcision wasn't about their convictions but about people-pleasing. Paul made it clear that we can't serve God and people simultaneously. One must cancel out the other.

Am I driven to meet the expectations of my parents? To prove people wrong? To get more followers and "likes"? Are there insecurities from the past that still surface as an adult, like some kind of revenge for getting picked last in kickball? We must ask God to search our hearts (Ps. 139:23–24). We must also be clear in our minds about what actually pleases the Lord. Doing something "for God" does not mean that ambition was pleasing to God.

How Is My Ambition Expressed?

We all know someone who has embarked on an entrepreneurial journey and whose personal social media pages have become endless sales pitches. Usually we can recognize that kind of ambition. Others are dreamers aiming for greatness. I know of one young man who was so dead set on making it big in Nashville that he pretended to move there and posted online from his parents' house (not in Nashville) with Nashville as the location tag.

Other times, people veil their ambition in religious tasks, aiming to be seen as righteous or pure. Or, more popular in new prosperity circles, some people make their apparent brokenness and vulnerability the brand of their social media "journey," and we are all there to follow along to see the crowds of people comment and share about how "real" and "authentic" the person is. Yes, Jesus loves even the friend of ours who is "extra"—whose Instagram posts we have to mute because they are exhaustingly self-absorbed. Jesus still loves the Christian who wants to be an influencer. But Jesus also gives us guidance on how to behave:

"Be careful not to practice your righteousness in front of others to be seen by them." (Matt. 6:1)
"But when you give to the poor, don't let your left hand know what your right hand is doing, so that your giving

may be in secret." (Matt. 6:3–4)

"When you pray, go into your private room, shut your door, and pray to your Father who is in secret." (Matt. 6:6)

"When you fast, put oil on your head and wash your face, so that your fasting isn't obvious to others but to your Father who is in secret." (Matt. 6:17–18)

Jesus is focused on our hearts. No amount of religious behavior could fool God or hide from Him our real motives. So it's in our best interest to evaluate our motives ourselves as well.

"Unholy ambition must be broken, or it will break us."[10] In my ambition, I hope my prayers consist less of "God, please grant me this" and more and more of "God, show me what You'd have me do. Be glorified in me." Let us pray as the psalmist did, "May the words of my mouth and the meditation of my heart be acceptable to you, LORD, my rock and my Redeemer" (Ps. 19:14).

13

Heavenly Minded, Earthly Good:

Is the Best Really Yet to Come?

Other joys do not fill the heart. But to know the Lord Jesus as our Surety satisfies the soul; it brings the soul unto rest under the eye of our pardoning God.
—ROBERT MURRAY M'CHEYNE

"The best is yet to come." I started this book by exploring the duality of a little phrase, and I'd like to end it the same way. Is "Christianity for losers," as Ted Turner believes? Yes and no. Is "the best yet to come" for Christians? By all means, yes. But not fully realized in this life.

So many Christians are taught to look past hardship and have more faith, clinging to promises that, with Jesus' victory in tow, "the best is yet to come." I can't help but wonder how this translated during COVID-19 when churches either could not gather for most of 2020 or returned to only a fraction of their pre-pandemic attendance. How did it translate to those who lost jobs during COVID-19 or experienced the death of a loved one to the virus and couldn't even be with them in the hospital to say goodbye?

Others didn't get to experience high school or college graduations, long-planned international mission trips, or their dream wedding. After my church's Easter service was canceled and we had to discontinue one of our church campuses indefinitely due to the pandemic and its aftermath, I might have found it very difficult to "maintain my Christian witness" (read: not punch something) if someone told me to believe more, because "the best is yet to come."

For those who don't know Christ, the best is usually not yet to come, even here on earth. People get older, feebler, and closer to death every day. The mortality rate in my city is 100% the last time I checked. For the unbeliever, this world is the best life will ever be. For the Christian, this world is the worst life will ever be. Jesus had His worst moment to ensure that the best actually is to come for His people. But I'm afraid the biblical context of this life versus the next just does not support the interpretation of "the best is yet to come" used by many Instagram celebrity pastors.

The promises of Christ are equally true of the believer locked in a jail cell for their faith and the Christian living in the suburbs scrolling through their social media feeds. But while the security and certainty of those promises are true at this very moment, the full realization is yet to come—in heaven, where we are fully united with Christ and with all creation sing His praises forever. Our best moments will be God-centered, rather than self-centered, as for all eternity we worship the Lamb who was slain. Our proclamation will be:

> **For the unbeliever, this world is the best life will ever be. For the Christian, this world is the worst life will ever be.**

Our Lord and God,
you are worthy to receive
glory and honor and power,
because you have created all things,
and by your will
they exist and were created. (Rev. 4:11)

Worthy is the Lamb who was slaughtered
to receive power and riches
and wisdom and strength
and honor and glory and blessing! . . .
Blessing and honor and glory and power
be to the one seated on the throne,
and to the Lamb, forever and ever! (Rev. 5:12–13)

This will be our best life. This is the best that is yet to come. If we're not careful, we can start believing the world's regular messaging about taking advantage of all this world has to offer because "you only live once (YOLO)." Combining this with church messaging about your best life now, there are times when heaven doesn't sound very exciting. Even though theologically I know that there will be no more tears, disease, or death in heaven and that sin will also be defeated, there are times this world can seem more enticing. In our relatively easy lives compared to many of our brothers and sisters around the world, it can be hard for so many of us to resonate with Paul's writing, "For we know that the whole creation has been groaning together with labor pains until now. Not only that, but we ourselves who have the Spirit as the firstfruits—we also groan within ourselves, eagerly waiting for adoption, the redemption of our bodies" (Rom. 8:22–23). If I'm honest, I like my house, my life, and still have some items on my bucket list that

I want to check off. It's so easy for even good things to become obstacles to true kingdom-mindedness. But I'm reminded of the Caedmon's Call song about the world having everything that I want but nothing that I actually need.

My least favorite Christian axiom is "Don't be so heavenly minded that you're no earthly good." When I read the Bible, I see that people who were the most heavenly minded actually did the most earthly good. In an earlier chapter, we looked at what is known as the Hall of Faith in Hebrews 11. After listing the names and acts of obedient faith they practiced in the name of the Lord, the author describes what drove them in their faithfulness: a home they did not receive here, a home that does not exist here.

They were so heavenly minded that they did much earthly good. Their motivation was the God who secures His promises, though they couldn't see the fruition of those promises. C. S. Lewis wrote, "If you read history you will find that the Christians who did most for the present world were just those who thought most of the next. . . . It is since Christians have largely ceased to think of the other world that they have become so ineffective in this."[1] I fear that not only does the new prosperity message mislead people, distracting them from kingdom effectiveness and true understanding of Christ, but it also makes heaven sound sort of like a letdown.

If you are living your best life now, why would you ever want that to end? If you are the center of the universe here, why would you want to go to a place that's all about Someone Else? When we look at the people listed in Hebrews, it is clear that this world mattered to them. They pursued faithfulness and had tremendous impact and influence on God's people. What strikes me is that they weren't looking for it. They were available, teachable, and faithful to the specific opportunities given them by the Lord.

The closing of Hebrews 11 has always struck me. When I read it slowly and ask the Lord to let me receive it into my heart as clearly as I can possibly comprehend, it points me away from myself completely: "All these were approved through their faith, but they did not receive what was promised, since God had provided something better for us" (Heb. 11:39–40). How easy is it to think that when something doesn't go as we wanted or planned that perhaps God didn't keep a promise to us? Perhaps in His timing it really is better for us to go without now for the collective fullness of joy later.

It wasn't that these people celebrated in Hebrews 11 were immune from crying out to God and asking why or how long the suffering and pain in their life was going to endure. If it were sinful to ask questions and wonder where God was in the events of their lives, the book of Psalms would be a strange inclusion in the canon of Scripture, and so would the major and minor prophets, and the writings of Paul. Yet the answer to their cries was never to believe in themselves more, or to wait for that big comeback, or to unlock potential inside. It was always to look to God and to the deliverer He was sending. The words immediately following the final verses of chapter 11 are these:

> Therefore, since we also have such a large cloud of witnesses surrounding us, let us lay aside every hindrance and the sin that so easily ensnares us. Let us run with endurance the race that lies before us, keeping our eyes on Jesus, the pioneer and perfecter of our faith. For the joy that lay before him, he endured the cross, despising the shame, and sat down at the right hand of the throne of God. (Heb. 12:1–2)

Let us look to those who went before us, but ultimately let us look to Christ—and not as a mere inspirational figure, but as one who endured the cross, rose again, and is now reigning and ruling.

Jesus is the ultimate fulfillment of God's promises. Scripture says that God the Father—who will not share His glory with another (Isa. 42:8)—was pleased to have all His fullness dwell in Jesus Christ (Col. 1:19).

It's clear that God is fully satisfied with Jesus. Am I? Can I truly say that what Christ accomplished is enough for my joy and contentment? Is there something else He needs to do to cover my needs? These are the questions we must ask ourselves about our faith. It's not enough to verbally disassociate ourselves from a new prosperity movement. We must test ourselves and see that the seeds of that thinking are not present or being watered in our own hearts. God's promises are yes in Christ, not in the desires of this world.

My primary impetus to write this book is not because I think hip, popular prosperity churches are having too much fun. It's because Jesus really is better than whatever else we could chase, and I don't want anyone to miss Him. Think of what's at the center of biblical Christianity versus what's at the center of me-centered Christianity. I am a flawed, sinful, inconsistent person who would make a terrible god. But the God of the Bible (and the universe, mind you) is glorious, pure, full of all power and wisdom, the inventor of joy and humor and music and pleasure and flavor and warmth and wonder and creativity. He is by every measure more worth pursuing than I am.

> **God's promises are yes in Christ, not in the desires of this world.**

Is there a place for believing that becoming a Christian or growing as a Christian does bring some life improvements? I would hope so! If we walk in the Spirit, we are told that we won't carry out the desires of the flesh (Gal. 5:16–17). In verse 19 of that chapter, Paul says the works of the flesh are "obvious." Some of those he lists are sexual immorality, moral impurity, and promiscuity. Just for starters, keeping away from sexual and moral sin as you walk with the Lord is a better life than what the world can offer. There's more. Jesus said that He wants us to have life in abundance (John 10:10). Immediately after those words He states that He, as the Good Shepherd, is going to lay His life down for His sheep. It is from the cross where an abundant life is understood. Here are some other practical benefits of following Christ:

There is joy for the person who considers others better than themselves.

Inner gratitude is displayed in generosity.

A Christian marriage is understood in self-sacrifice, submission, and by the portrait of the oneness between Christ and the church.

In the church there is encouragement and spurring on one another to good deeds.

Parenting as a Christian is purposeful, focusing on a child's heart more than basic moral conformity.

Those in dating relationships can see one another as brothers and sisters in Christ, rather than temporary partners to satisfy physical desires.

Fleeing from drunkenness keeps one from potential destructive decisions.

Understanding forgiveness in Christ fuels a refusal to hold on to grudges and bitterness.

There is hope and purpose in suffering.

Death is not final.

The Christian life truly is the best life now, because it roots itself in a person, Jesus Christ, who redeemed us into a life that is not of this world.

So how do we embrace the abundant life available to us in Christ?

1. Ask God to help you be gospel-centered.

Let the actual purposes of Christ be the driving force of your life. It is one thing to believe the gospel, and that's obviously of first and most importance (1 Cor. 15:1–3), but to find joy in the life of abundance that Jesus offers is to believe the gospel covers every area of our lives. Yes, it saves, but it also sanctifies and sustains. Jesus' saving work is the message; it is the point. Does a sermon you hear on a Sunday give you more confidence in Christ or more confidence in yourself? Jesus is the hero of the entire Bible, so He should be the hero and the point of every sermon. We proclaim Him. Jesus is the means, and He is the end.

2. By grace, through Scripture, seek to increase your knowledge of God.

Knowledge intake for the sake of knowledge alone is not the way of the Christian, as Paul warned that it "puffs up" (1 Cor. 8:1). Knowledge of God is deficient if it doesn't first grow our affections for God. Affections for God that are based on emotional worship experiences can be genuine, but when the lights go out, the fog clears, and the auditorium empties, the only thing you can hope is that the best is yet to come. Growing in your knowledge of God's character, Christ's person, and His promises, however, reminds you as a Christian that on this side of eternity, the best is already here, and that's a wonderful realization. Our growing knowledge of God means a greater knowledge of His Word. That is how He has chosen to speak to us and inform us of who He is, who we are, and what He has done for His people.

To silence all of the messaging trying to convince us that we write our own stories, we must be in the Scriptures daily. The reason why John the Baptist, at the height of his attention and fanfare, could deflect misplaced hype and point people to Jesus was because of his knowledge of who had actually arrived on the scene. It was the Messiah, the Son of God, the Lamb of God who takes away the sins of the world (John 1:29).

> **To silence all of the messaging trying to convince us that we write our own stories, we must be in the Scriptures daily.**

Based on his knowledge of who Jesus was and what He came to do, the only logical response was John's insistence, "He must increase, but I must decrease" (John 3:30). The new prosperity gospel is fine with Christ increasing, as long as the individual gets to increase with Him. But as our knowledge of the Scriptures increases, we learn there is no room for both. Our desire to advance ourselves alongside Jesus is as old as the Last Supper (Luke 22:24–30), the illusion of human superiority goes back even farther to the Tower of Babel, and the desire to be like God and no longer need to submit to Him all started in the garden of Eden.

As we read and study the Bible, we will learn more about God and His character and be sure of the promises He has made to His people. This gives us peace of mind as we live in the "not yet" of the final realization of those promises while enjoying the "already" of those promises by living our life with God. We have a church member who first walked in our door as a college student. He was invited by a friend, and up to the time he entered our church, his experience with local churches and pastors was all new prosperity. After he made some friendships and started discipleship in our church, something radically changed in him. He started learning theology and doctrine. In other words, he started reading his Bible, not just his page-long devotional, but actually reading the Scriptures. Verse by verse, and letter by letter. Today he has some of the strongest gospel convictions of any college student I've ever met, along with a passion to reach others for Christ. It changes everything.

Eventually, you become equipped to recognize when what a pastor is selling doesn't line up with the framework of the Scriptures. Our Creator wants us to know who He is, and the Scriptures are the means by which He tells us all He wants us to know about Himself.

3. Pursue the ordinary life.

Author Michael Horton describes a troubling aspect of American Christianity as "an impatience and disdain for the ordinary."[2] The norm is for Christians to be pushed to make life-changing choices and "trail-blaze new paths to greatness."[3] Robert Davis Smart summarizes Horton's book: "'Super-apostles,' heroes, and gospel celebrities are not needed, nor even helpful. Rather, what is needed, is the courage to live out one's calling as a member in a local church that practices the right use of the ordinary means of grace with continuity for a long time towards maturity."[4] I truly believe the pathway to an abundant life is one that could easily be viewed as basic or ordinary.

It is in the daily routine where disciples are made and our actual selves, off-camera and no filters, are present. We live in a society where minivans are mocked, the slightest appearance of a gray hair causes a panic, and anything we can possibly do to project a non-ordinary life is the goal of each day. Yet Jesus was so unimpressive by the expectations of His surrounding culture that when He first came into public ministry, people couldn't get over where He was from. "Can anything good come out of Nazareth?" (John 1:46). It is hard to follow Jesus when your life is in Nazareth, but you want the world to think it is Manhattan. The reality is, most Christians are going to live a life that resembles Manhattan, Kansas, more than New York. The abundant life is one that makes the ordinary things extraordinary because life with God, family, and the church on His mission is exactly what He designed.

4. Find godly community.

One of my mentors used to say, "People aren't looking for a friendly church, they are looking for friends." Every church claims to be a friendly church because Ms. Betty passes out bulletins each Sunday and is the sweetest lady of all time. But people are looking for true community, and that is a God-given desire, a righteous and pure longing. The local church is the spiritual family of the believer and should be a major component of the abundant life. We bear with one another, but even more, we follow Jesus together.

Charles Spurgeon called the local church the "dearest place."[5] Where else can people of all ages, colors, personality types, vocations, and backgrounds come together united by love and committed to a lifelong pursuit of selflessness? If fellow local church members commit to support and encourage one another as outlined in the Scriptures rather than compete against each other for trendiness and worldly marks of approval, you'll find a special kind of steadfast community that transcends anything else in this life. In a church family, the last thing you should have to do is prove yourself or feel any pressure to be savvy or cool to belong. Any pressure, spoken or unspoken, to look a certain way to be part of a church's culture is of the world, not the church of Jesus Christ.

5. Pray for willingness to be marginalized.

There is nothing, absolutely nothing, one can do to make the gospel and biblical ethics more appealing to people who think it is foolishness. It is like handing a pork sandwich to a committed vegan. It doesn't matter how much barbeque sauce or what kinds of delicious fixings are under the bun; it's still pork. The only way they're eating the sandwich is if you swap that hog with tofu. That's what we would have to do to sound doctrine to make the world love it: deny it altogether.

We can't make Christianity cooler. The attempts have been made, and eventually those churches fade off to oblivion or wind up denying foundational truths of the Bible. Are you willing to be marginalized for the sake of Christ and His Word? There is an abundant life following Jesus down the narrow road, because it is a life with God. We must hold to the faith that has been delivered to the saints once and for all (Jude 3) and believe that true life is found in God. Are you willing to say that Jesus is the only way of salvation? Are you willing to hold to the foundational biblical truth that marriage is between a man and a woman? Are you willing to tell a Christian friend you don't approve of her upcoming wedding because you love her and believe her divorce was unbiblical?

The narrow way means sometimes your earthly experience will not feel victorious. These views will marginalize. It is hard to claim "the best is yet to come" when a professing Christian friend no longer speaks to you because you don't embrace his adult son's homosexual lifestyle. We don't boast in situations where our faith separates us from others, nor do we take pleasure, but the abundant life Jesus promised comes from standing in agreement with our Savior, not at odds with Him, on all matters of Scripture. We must be willing to ask what He wants us to do (through His Word) and to do it. No matter the cost. He knows how to make people flourish, and it's not by following the desires of our hearts.

We are a people who have been rescued. From death to life. We stand on the side of Jesus with compassion, knowing we are like the ones Paul spoke of, saying, "And some of you used to be like this. But you were washed, you were sanctified, you were justified in the name of the Lord Jesus Christ and by the Spirit of our God" (1 Cor. 6:11). We stand firm in our convictions and offer an earnest invitation to join us in pursuit of Christ. He died so that those who live no longer live for themselves but for Him who died and rose from the grave (2 Cor. 5:15). The two efforts can't coexist. God have mercy on us—we need a reckoning concerning who exactly is the point of the Scriptures. It is not me; it is not you. His name is Jesus.

His glory is our reward.

Acknowledgments

This book came out of a passion I have for gospel-centrality and a great concern for those missing out on it by embracing the new prosperity gospel and its self-focused message. I'm grateful for the many Sunday night conversations at my house working through ideas and concerns that led me to write this book. Thank you to those who have sat in my living room and helped identify the new prosperity problem and encouraged me to pursue this project, mainly Brian Seagraves, Hunter Leavine, Jordan Priddle, and David Kirkpatrick.

I am thankful for Todd Doss, the leader of our music at City Church. He is committed to choosing songs for our congregation that come from trusted, gospel-preaching churches, rather than expose our church family to artists and other churches that could lead them theologically and biblically astray. It matters deeply, and Todd is a man of great conviction and a heart for the shepherding of the church.

Giana Hall is one of the most gifted writers I know. She reads my words before anyone else sees them, and I'm grateful for her work in helping this book come together. It is a blessing to have a hometown editor in our local church, and also in my life as a great friend. Thank you, G!

I continue to be grateful for the opportunities given to me by Erik Wolgemuth, Drew Dyck, and Moody Publishers to be able to write books for the church and to speak into matters of great importance. Thank you to Mackenzie Conway for her expertise and oversight of this book.

I also thank the Lord that I get to serve as the pastor of City Church in Tallahassee. I love the local church, and I especially love ours. It is a great joy of my life to serve with the staff and elders and minister together for the gospel and for the city.

Notes

CHAPTER 1
Loserville: Is Christianity for the Cool, Trendy, and Successful?

Epigraph: Fred B. Craddock, *As One without Authority: Fourth Edition Revised and with New Sermons* (St. Louis: Chalice Press, 2001), 11.
1. Immanuel Nashville (@ImmanuelNash), Twitter, August 8, 2019, https://twitter.com/ImmanuelNash/status/1163128059064651776?s=20.

CHAPTER 2
The Shenanigans: What Goes On Inside a New Prosperity Church

1. Carl R. Trueman, "Kissing Christianity Goodbye," *First Things*, July 30, 2019, https://www.firstthings.com/web-exclusives/2019/07/kissing-christianity-goodbye.
2. Trevin Wax, "Don't Settle for the Gospel of Self-Fulfillment," The Gospel Coalition, November 28, 2016, https://www.thegospelcoalition.org/blogs/trevin-wax/dont-settle-for-the-gospel-of-self-fulfillment/.
3. Ibid.
4. Conrad Mbewe, "'Jesus Died for Sinners': Do Your People Know What This Actually Means?," 9Marks, August 20, 2019, https://www.9marks.org/article/jesus-died-for-sinners-do-your-people-know-what-this-actually-means/.

CHAPTER 3
What's the Hype?: The Draw of Worldly Christianity

Epigraph: Leonard Ravenhill, *Revival God's Way: A Message for the Church* (1983; repr., Grand Rapids, MI: Bethany House Publishers, 2006), 57.
1. Jen Pollock Michel, "Glennon Doyle Melton's Gospel of Self-Fulfillment," *Christianity Today*, November 20, 2016, https://www.christianitytoday.com/ct/2016/november-web-only/glennon-doyle-meltons-gospel-of-self-fulfillment.html.
2. Mark Sayers, *Disappearing Church: From Cultural Relevance to Gospel Resilience* (Chicago: Moody Publishers, 2016), 83.
3. Steven Furtick, *Sun Stand Still: What Happens When You Dare to Ask God for the Impossible* (Colorado Springs: Multnomah Books, 2010), 7.
4. Steven Furtick, *Greater: Dream Bigger. Start Smaller. Ignite God's Vision for Your Life* (Colorado Springs: Multnomah Books, 2012), 30.
5. Ibid., 157.
6. Now, to be fair, sometimes even the most conservative, Reformed congregations will also feel that a particular gathering was powerful or moving, and we may even say that the Holy Spirit was at work. But we believe the Holy Spirit is also at work

in the quiet, private moments of difficult discipleship and daily duties of obeying the Lord.

7. Tara Isabella Burton, *Strange Rites: New Religions for a Godless World* (New York: PublicAffairs, 2020), 94.

8. Costi W. Hinn (@costiwhinn), Twitter, January 1, 2020, https://twitter.com/costiwhinn/status/1212441591207456768.

9. Bob Dylan, "When You Gonna Wake Up?," *Slow Train Coming*, Columbia Records, 1979.

10. Jon Bloom, "What Jesus Meant When He Said, 'You Must Eat My Flesh,'" Desiring God, June 3, 2008, https://www.desiringgod.org/articles/what-jesus-meant-when-he-said-you-must-eat-my-flesh.

11. Ibid.

12. Ibid.

13. Jared C. Wilson (@jaredcwilson), Twitter, August 29, 2019, https://twitter.com/jaredcwilson/status/1167143127364362240.

CHAPTER 4

Hashtag Filter: The Promise of the Socially Approved Life

Epigraph: Owen Strachan (@ostrachan), Twitter, August 27, 2020, https://twitter.com/ostrachan/status/1299003627894460416.

1. Christian Smith and Melinda Lundquist Denton, *Soul Searching: The Religious and Spiritual Lives of American Teenagers* (New York: Oxford University Press, 2009), 163.

2. Brian Cosby, "Moral Therapeutic Deism: Not Just a Problem with Youth Ministry," The Gospel Coalition, April 9, 2012, https://www.thegospelcoalition.org/article/mtd-not-just-a-problem-with-youth-ministry/.

3. Jared C. Wilson, *The Gospel According to Satan: Eight Lies about God That Sound Like the Truth* (Nashville: Nelson Books, 2020).

4. Sarah Young. *Jesus Calling: Enjoying Peace in His Presence* (Nashville: Thomas Nelson, 2004), 87.

5. Ibid., 6.

6. Ibid., p. xii.

7. Kenda Creasy Dean, *Almost Christian: What the Faith of Our Teenagers Is Telling the American Church* (New York: Oxford University Press, 2010), 29.

8. Cosby, "Moral Therapeutic Deism."

9. Ibid.

10. Michael Reeves, *Rejoice and Tremble: The Surprising Good News of the Fear of the Lord* (Wheaton, IL: Crossway, 2021), 19.

11. Rusty McKie, "Don't Expect a Spectacular Christian Life," The Gospel Coalition, November 21, 2017, https://www.thegospelcoalition.org/article/dont-expect-spectacular-christian-life/.

12. John Flavel, *The Works of John Flavel* (Edinburgh: The Banner of Truth Trust, 1968), 6:84.

CHAPTER 5

This Is So Boring: The New Prosperity Cardinal Sin of Settling for the Mundane

Epigraph: Charles Spurgeon, "Strangers and Sojourners," *The Metropolitan Tabernacle Pulpit*, sermon delivered November 5, 1863, Metropolitan Tabernacle,

Newington, published January 26, 1911, Spurgeon Gems, https://www
.spurgeongems.org/sermon/chs3234.pdf.

1. Skye Jethani, *What If Jesus Was Serious? A Visual Guide to the Teachings of Jesus We Love to Ignore* (Chicago: Moody Publishers, 2020), 85.

2. Rachel Hollis, *Girl, Wash Your Face: Stop Believing the Lies About Who You Are So You Can Become Who You Were Meant to Be* (Nashville: Thomas Nelson, 2018), 5, xi, 31.

3. Alisa Childers, "Girl, Wash Your Face? What Rachel Hollis Gets Right and Wrong," The Gospel Coalition, September 24, 2018, https://www.thegospelcoalition.org/reviews/girl-wash-face/.

4. Ibid.

5. Jen Oshman, "Girl, Follow Jesus," The Gospel Coalition, March 4, 2019, https://www.thegospelcoalition.org/reviews/girl-stop-apologizing/.

6. Rachel Hollis, *Girl, Stop Apologizing: A Shame-Free Plan for Embracing and Achieving Your Goals* (Nashville: HarperCollins Leadership, 2019), 83.

7. Oshman, "Girl, Follow Jesus."

8. Ibid.

9. Ibid.

10. Childers, "Girl, Wash Your Face?"

11. Matt Smethurst, Tim Keller, and Kathy Keller, "Tim and Kathy Keller on Dating, Marriage, Complementarianism, and Other Small Topics," The Gospel Coalition, October 24, 2019, https://www.thegospelcoalition.org/article/tim-kathy-keller-marriage/.

12. Jason Helopoulos, "Contentment in a Discontented World," The Gospel Coalition, February 17, 2017, https://www.thegospelcoalition.org/blogs/kevin-deyoung/contentment-in-a-discontented-world/.

13. Ibid.

14. J. Ligon Duncan, June 1, 2008, First Presbyterian Church, "Content in Every Situation," sermon, Jackson, Mississippi, https://ligonduncan.com/content-in-every-situation-706/.

15. Chris Tomlin, "Enough," Not to Us, Six Step Records, 2002.

CHAPTER 6

Mum's the Word: Lite on Doctrine and Theology as a Means to Grow the Church

Epigraph: Jen Wilkin, *Women of the Word: How to Study the Bible with Both Our Hearts and Our Minds* (Wheaton, IL: Crossway, 2014), 31.

1. Aaron Armstrong, "Sound Doctrine," The Gospel Coalition, May 15, 2013, https://www.thegospelcoalition.org/reviews/sound-doctrine/.

2. Robert B. Jamieson III, *Sound Doctrine: How a Church Grows in the Love and Holiness of God* (Wheaton, IL: Crossway, 2013), 85.

3. Armstrong, "Sound Doctrine."

4. Ibid.

5. Ibid.

6. Scott Swain, "What Is Sound Doctrine?," *Ligonier*, January 27, 2017, https://www.ligonier.org/blog/what-doctrine/.

7. John M. Frame, "Virgin Birth of Christ," in *Evangelical Dictionary of Theology*, 2nd ed., Walter A. Elwell, ed. (Grand Rapids, MI: Baker Academic, 2001), 1249–50.

8. Bryan Litfin, "Why We Need More Pastors Like Augustine: Retrieving Ancient Pastoral Practice," The Gospel Coalition, June 24, 2019, https://www.thegospelcoalition.org/article/more-pastors-augustine/.

9. Kevin DeYoung, "Is Theology Theoretical or Practical?," The Gospel Coalition, January 16, 2014, https://www.thegospelcoalition.org/blogs/kevin-deyoung/is-theology-theoretical-or-practical/.

10. Francis Turretin, *Institutes of Elenctic Theology*, ed. James T. Dennison Jr., trans. George Musgrave Giger (Phillipsburg, NJ: P&R Publishing, 1992), 1:21.

11. DeYoung, "Is Theology Theoretical or Practical?"

CHAPTER 7
All Hat, No Cattle: The False Advertisement of New Prosperity Churches

Epigraph: C. H. Spurgeon, *The Soul-Winner; or, How to Lead Sinners to the Saviour* (New York: Fleming H. Revell Co., 1895), 14.

1. Mark Galli, "Do I Have a Witness?," *Christianity Today*, October 4, 2007, https://www.christianitytoday.com/ct/2007/octoberweb-only/140-42.0.html.

2. Ibid.

3. Jared C. Wilson, "What You Win Them With Is What You Win Them To," *The Gospel-Driven Church* (blog), October 5, 2007, http://gospeldrivenchurch.blogspot.com/2007/10/what-you-win-them-with-is-what-you-win.html.

4. Ibid.

5. John Starke (@john_starke), Twitter, July 22, 2020, https://twitter.com/john_starke/status/1286020267643461635?s=20.

6. Dane Ortlund, *Gentle and Lowly: The Heart of Christ for Sinners and Sufferers* (Wheaton, IL: Crossway, 2020), 186.

7. Francis James Grimké, *The Works of Francis J. Grimke*, Carter G. Woodson, ed. (Associated Publishers, Incorporated, 1942), 33.

8. Jared C. Wilson, "The Attractional Church's Trojan Rabbit," The Gospel Coalition, October 25, 2017, https://www.thegospelcoalition.org/blogs/jared-c-wilson/attractional-churchs-trojan-rabbit/.

9. Mike Cosper, "Kill Your (Celebrity Culture) Worship," The Gospel Coalition, January 29, 2016, https://www.thegospelcoalition.org/article/kill-your-celebrity-culture-worship/.

10. Aaron Armstrong, "Crash the Chatterbox: Hearing God's Voice Above All Others," The Gospel Coalition, September 10, 2014, https://www.thegospelcoalition.org/reviews/crash-chatterbox/.

11. Cosper, "Kill Your (Celebrity Culture) Worship."

CHAPTER 8
Context Is King: How Selective Bible Verses Fuel the Movement

Epigraph: Carly Simon, "You're So Vain," *No Secrets*, Elektra Records, 1972.

1. Christopher J. H. Wright, *The Mission of God: Unlocking the Bible's Grand Narrative* (Downers Grove, IL: InterVarsity Press, 2006), 533–34.

2. Joel Osteen (@JoelOsteen), Twitter, April 12, 2020, https://twitter.com/JoelOsteen/status/1249526472131465216.

3. Nancy Guthrie, "Nancy Guthrie on How God Gives Christians the Desires of Their Hearts," The Gospel Coalition, March 20, 2019, https://www

.thegospelcoalition.org/video/nancy-guthrie-god-gives-christians-desires-hearts/.

4. David Powlison, *Seeing with New Eyes: Counseling and the Human Condition through the Lens of Scripture* (Phillipsburg, NJ: P&R Publishing, 2003), 148.
5. Ibid.
6. Russell Moore, "Does Jeremiah 29:11 Apply to You?," RussellMoore.com, June 28, 2017, https://www.russellmoore.com/2017/06/28/jeremiah-2911-apply/.
7. Ibid.
8. Ibid.

CHAPTER 9
Sharing the Spotlight: Pursuing Greater Things for Ourselves "in Jesus' Name"

1. "About the Book," http://greaterbook.com/about.
2. Matt Fuller, *Be True to Yourself: Why It Doesn't Mean What You Think It Does (and How That Can Make You Happy)* (Epsom, England: The Good Book Company, 2020), 37.
3. Don Carson, "How We Do Greater Things Than Jesus," The Gospel Coalition, April 2, 2018, https://www.thegospelcoalition.org/article/how-do-great-things-jesus/.
4. Ibid.
5. D. A. Carson, "Seek Thou Great Things for Thyself?," *Themelios* 41, no. 3, https://www.thegospelcoalition.org/themelios/article/seekest-thou-great-things-for-thyself/.
6. Ibid.
7. Ibid.
8. Fuller, *Be True to Yourself.*
9. Jon Bloom, "Pleasure Is the Measure of Your Treasure," Desiring God, September 16, 2011, https://www.desiringgod.org/articles/pleasure-is-the-measure-of-your-treasure.
10. Erik Raymond, "The Self Interest of God (Psalm 117)," The Gospel Coalition, May 4, 2006, https://www.thegospelcoalition.org/blogs/erik-raymond/the-self-interest-of-god-psalm-117/.
11. Dane Ortlund, "What's All This 'Gospel-Centered' Talk About?," *Boundless*, July 14, 2014, https://www.boundless.org/faith/whats-all-this-gospel-centered-talk-about/.
12. "Glossary: Theology of Glory," *Mockingbird*, https://mbird.com/glossary/theology-of-glory/.
13. Ibid.
14. George Eldon Ladd, *The Gospel of the Kingdom: Scriptural Studies in the Kingdom of God* (Eastford, CT: Martino Fine Books, 2011), 128.
15. Scott Hubbard, "God Will Daily Bear You Up," Desiring God, July 17, 2019, https://www.desiringgod.org/articles/god-will-daily-bear-you-up.
16. Jerry Bridges, *The Pursuit of Holiness* (Colorado Springs: NavPress, 2016), 4.
17. TobyMac, Instagram, October 24, 2019, https://www.instagram.com/p/B4BBfFcBeMg/?utm_source=ig_embed.

CHAPTER 10
Curb Your Enthusiasm: The Unmet Expectations of the New Prosperity
Gospel

Epigraph: Quoted in Janet and Geoff Benge, *Count Zinzendorf: Firstfruit*, Christian
    Heroes: Then & Now (Seattle: YWAM Publishing, 2006), 102.
  1. Melissa Kruger, "Evaluating Our Expectations: The American Dream vs.
     the Christian's Hope," The Gospel Coalition, July 4, 2017,
     https://www.thegospelcoalition.org/blogs/melissa-kruger/evaluating-our-
     expectations-the-american-dream-vs-the-christians-hope/.
  2. Jackie Knapp, "What If Your 20s Weren't What You Expected?," The Gospel
     Coalition, May 16, 2014, https://www.thegospelcoalition.org/article/what-if-
     your-20s-werent-what-you-expected/.
  3. Matt Perman, "Was William Carey Being Biblical When He Said 'Expect Great
     Things from God'?," February 21, 2011, https://mattperman.com/2011/02/
     was-william-carey-being-biblical-when-he-said-expect-great-things-from-god/.
  4. Ibid.
  5. William Carey, *An Enquiry into the Obligations of Christians to Use Means for the
     Conversion of the Heathens* (Leicester, England: Ann Ireland, 1792), 8. https://
     www.wmcarey.edu/carey/enquiry/anenquiry.pdf.
  6. William Carey, 1792, quoted in "William Carey," *Christian History* (1992),
     Christianity Today, https://www.christianitytoday.com/history/people/mis-
     sionaries/william-carey.html.
  7. Guy M. Richard, "Expect Great Things from God," *Tabletalk*, December 27, 2019,
     https://tabletalkmagazine.com/posts/expect-great-things-from-god-2019-12/.
  8. Erik Raymond, "Are You All In on the Promises of God?," The Gospel Coalition,
     May 4, 2017, https://www.thegospelcoalition.org/blogs/erik-raymond/are-you-
     all-in-on-the-promises-of-god/.

CHAPTER 11
The Great Escape: Aftermath of Pop-Christian Discipleship

Epigraph: Alex Kocman, "Be Christ-Centered, Not Just Gospel-Centered," *Alex
    Kocman* (blog), March 16, 2019, https://alexkocman.com/2019/03/16/be-
    christ-centered-not-just-gospel-centered/.
  1. Ray Ortlund, *The Gospel: How the Church Portrays the Beauty of Christ* (Wheaton,
     IL: Crossway, 2014), 18.
  2. Amy Gannett, "Stop Eating Spiritual Candy," The Gospel Coalition, February 25,
     2019, https://www.thegospelcoalition.org/article/stop-eating-spiritual-candy/.
  3. Ibid.
  4. John Owen, *The Glory of Christ* (Chicago: Moody Publishers, 1949).
  5. Joe Thorn, "Gospel Centered," JoeThorn.net, August 11, 2009, http://www
     .joethorn.net/2009/08/11/gospel-centered/.
  6. Ibid.
  7. Kocman, "Be Christ-Centered, Not Just Gospel-Centered," (blog), March 16,
     2019.
  8. John Stott, *The Message of Ephesians*, The Bible Speaks Today (Leicester, England:
     Inter-Varsity Press, 1984), 128–30.

9. "False Signs and Wonders," *Tabletalk*, October 10, 2016, https:// tabletalkmagazine.com/daily-study/2016/10/false-signs-and-wonders/.

10. Owen Strachan, "Reasons Why I Did Not Convert to Christianity," Reformanda, February 14, 2020, https://www.reformandamin.org/articles1/2020/2/14/ reasons-why-i-did-not-convert-to-christianity.

11. David F. Wells, *The Courage to Be Protestant: Truth-lovers, Marketers, and Emergents in the Postmodern World* (Grand Rapids, MI: Eerdmans, 2008), 49–50.

12. Kyle Strobel and Jamin Goggin, "Why Christians Should Be Cautious of Self-Help Resources," The Gospel Coalition, October 23, 2019, https://www.thegospelcoalition.org/video/christians-cautious-self-help-resources/.

13. Ibid.

14. Trevin Wax, "No Meat or Potatoes, but the Candy Aisle Is Full," The Gospel Coalition, March 17, 2020, https://www.thegospelcoalition.org/blogs/trevin-wax/no-meat-and-potatoes-but-the-candy-aisle-is-full/.

15. Amie Patrick, "Self-Care and Self-Denial," The Gospel Coalition, August 10, 2015, https://www.thegospelcoalition.org/article/self-care-and-self-denial/.

16. Jennifer Beer, "The Inconvenient Truth about Your 'Authentic' Self," *Scientific American*, March 5, 2020, https://blogs.scientificamerican.com/observations/the-inconvenient-truth-about-your-authentic-self/.

17. Emma Scrivener, "The Problem with 'Authentic,'" *A New Name* (blog), April 30, 2017, https://emmascrivener.net/2017/04/the-problem-with-authentic/.

18. Ibid.

19. Ibid.

20. Tony Merida, "Your Church Might Not Be as Gospel-Centered as You Think," The Gospel Coalition, April 10, 2018, https://www.thegospelcoalition.org/article/your-church-gospel-centered-think/.

21. Ibid.

22. Ibid.

23. Tim Keller, "What Is Gospel-Centered Ministry?," The Gospel Coalition, May 28, 2007, https://www.thegospelcoalition.org/conference_media/gospel-centered-ministry/.

24. Martyn Lloyd-Jones, *The Puritans: Their Origins and Successors* (London: Banner of Truth, 2014), 360.

CHAPTER 12
Most Likely to Succeed: Pursuing Godly Ambition

Epigraph: Bart Barber (@bartbarber), Twitter, May 8, 2020, https://twitter.com/bartbarber/status/1258949818078068738.

1. Dan Dodds, "The Place of Godly Ambition," *Tabletalk*, October 2018, https://tabletalkmagazine.com/article/2018/10/place-godly-ambition/.

2. Matt Smethurst, "What God Values More Than Your Motives," The Gospel Coalition, September 16, 2015, https://www.thegospelcoalition.org/article/what-god-values-more-than-your-motives/.

3. Jon Bloom, "Escaping the Slavery of Selfish Ambition," Desiring God, May 23, 2014, https://www.desiringgod.org/articles/escaping-the-slavery-of-selfish-ambition.

4. Chuck Colson, quoted in "Ambition," Bible in One Year, Day 275, https://
   bibleinoneyear.org/bioy/commentary/654. Portions of this quote are italicized
   in the cited source.
5. Bruce Baugus, "The Disease of Ambition," *Reformation21*, January 14, 2019,
   https://www.reformation21.org/blogs/the-disease-of-ambition.php.
6. Ibid.
7. John Piper, "Is Love of Money Really the Root of All Evils?," Desiring God,
   February 7, 2017, https://www.desiringgod.org/articles/is-love-of-money-
   really-the-root-of-all-evils.
8. Kristen Wetherell, "Is It Right for Christians to Be Ambitious?," *Crosswalk*,
   March 31, 2015, https://www.crosswalk.com/family/career/is-it-right-for-
   christians-to-be-ambitious.html.
9. Eric Geiger, "3 Questions to Test Your Ambition," *Eric Geiger* (blog), September
   12, 2019, https://ericgeiger.com/2019/09/3-questions-to-test-your-ambition/.
10. Ibid.

CHAPTER 13

Heavenly Minded, Earthly Good: Is the Best Really Yet to Come?

Epigraph: Quoted in Andrew A. Bonar, *Memoir and Remains of the Rev. Robert Murray
   M'Cheyne* (Edinburgh & London: Oliphant Anderson & Ferrier, 1892), 286.
1. C. S. Lewis, *Mere Christianity* (1952; repr., New York: HarperOne, 2001), 134.
2. Michael Horton, *Ordinary: Sustainable Faith in a Radical, Restless World* (Grand
   Rapids, MI: Zondervan, 2014), 18.
3. Ibid., 12.
4. Robert Davis Smart, review of *Ordinary: Sustainable Faith in a Radical, Restless
   World* by Michael Horton, *Themelios* 40, no. 3 (December 2015), https://www
   .thegospelcoalition.org/themelios/review/ordinary-sustainable-faith-in-a-
   radical-restless-world-michael-horton/.
5. Charles Spurgeon, "The Best Donation," *The Metropolitan Tabernacle Pulpit*,
   sermon delivered April 5, 1891, Metropolitan Tabernacle, Newington, Spurgeon
   Gems, http://www.spurgeongems.org/sermon/chs2234.pdf.

HOW TO REACH CULTURAL CHRISTIANS
WHO DON'T REALLY KNOW JESUS

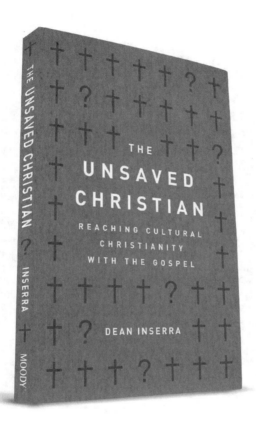

MOODY
Publishers®

From the Word to Life®

The Unsaved Christian equips you to confront cultural
Christianity with honesty, compassion, and grace,
whether you're doing it from the pulpit or the pews.
If you've ever felt stuck or unsure how to minister to
someone who identifies as Christian but still needs
Jesus, this book is for you.

978-0-8024-1880-7 | also available as eBook and audiobook

DOUBTING GOD IS NORMAL.
BUT CONFIDENCE IN HIM IS POSSIBLE.